Why Does the Devil Want Our Souls?

Komlan Ahoudou

Table of Contents

Dedication

To the seekers of truth: those who dare to question, ponder, and delve into the mysteries of existence. To those, too, who find solace and inspiration in the ongoing dialogue between humanity and the Divine. This work is dedicated to you, the intrepid explorers of the soul's journey, whose unwavering curiosity fuels the flame of understanding. May these pages offer a spark of insight into the intricate tapestry of life, and into the profound significance of our choices. May they reflect the enduring power of the human spirit, which strives for meaning and purpose amidst the complexities of existence. For within each of us resides a spark of the Divine, a potential for boundless growth and transformation waiting to be awakened and nurtured.

This book is a testament to that boundless potential that lies ahead, which is grounded in the enduring hope that guides our steps along life's challenging path. It is a tribute to the human capacity, which embraces uncertainty and finds meaning in the face of the unknown. It is also a celebration of the individual's relentless pursuit of knowledge and understanding, and a dedication to the enduring quest over a life lived with purpose and fulfillment. May this exploration inspire you to further your own journey of self-discovery and spiritual growth.

Preface

This book embarks on a unique theological and philosophical exploration. It seeks to reimagine a familiar narrative about the devil's alleged desire for human souls. Here, we move beyond the simplistic portrayal of pure malevolence, and instead frame this desire as a reflection of the profound and intrinsic connection between humanity and the divine.

Our journey focuses on the soul's trajectory, not just from birth to death but also from a possible pre-existent state, through the complexities of earthly existence, and ultimately towards its ultimate destiny. We delve into the concept of fulfilling one's purpose, one that transcends the simple pursuit of happiness. This book challenges the reader to consider the often-conflicting forces of duty and personal aspiration, and the implications of our choices on our spiritual path.

This is not a straightforward theological treatise, but a narrative exploration that uses theological and philosophical frameworks, to examine fundamental questions about life, purpose, and the relationship between humanity and the divine. The exploration of the devil's desire serves as a metaphorical lens, through which we examine the deep-seated human longing for something greater, something beyond the mundane - something that resonates with the universal aspiration for meaning and connection.

The narrative will challenge your assumptions and invite you to reflect on your own journey towards spiritual fulfillment. This work is not designed to offer definitive answers, but rather to take you through a journey of questions and ongoing exploration.

It takes a path that should provoke thought, foster deeper self-awareness, and ultimately inspire a more meaningful life.

Introduction

Our understanding of the human condition is perpetually shaped by the narratives we create and the questions we ask. This book engages with a timeless narrative, which encompasses the struggle between good and evil as often personified in the conflict between humanity and some malevolent force.

However, we approach this age-old story from a fresh perspective, reframing the traditional understanding of the devil's desire for souls. We posit that this "desire," rather than representing pure antagonism, symbolizes a profound truth: the inherent connection between humanity and the Divine. Within this interpretation, the devil's pursuit represents the persistent tug-of-war within the human soul – a yearning for something beyond the material even as the desire for vanity persists; a longing for purpose and fulfillment that echoes the divine spark within each of us. This book explores the soul's journey not simply from birth to death, but as a process that is potentially eternal.

We consider the possibility of the soul's pre-existence, its entry into the physical realm, the complexities of navigating the earthly life with its inherent challenges and conflicts, and finally, the soul's ultimate destination. We examine the concept of one's sense of duty, and its often-conflicting relationship with personal desires. We also examine the profound impact our choices have on our spiritual trajectory.

The book is structured to engage both theological and philosophical considerations. We will draw upon diverse religious traditions and philosophical schools of thought, to create a rich tapestry of perspectives on the soul's journey. This is not a simplistic narrative of good versus evil, but a nuanced exploration of human experience that examines the interplay between free will and fate, the struggle between personal aspiration and a sense of duty, and the ongoing quest for meaning within a larger cosmic design. Prepare for a journey that will challenge your assumptions, provoke your thinking, and ultimately inspire you to contemplate your own place within the grand narrative of existence.

The Divine Blueprint: Understanding Our Inherent Nature

The very notion of a soul, its creation, and its inherent nature has captivated humankind for millennia. Across diverse religious and philosophical traditions, the concept of a soul—that ethereal

essence that is the animating principle of life—has been interpreted in countless ways. Yet a common thread persists. The soul is not merely a byproduct of biological processes; it is an entity imbued with deeper significance. It is connected to something transcendent, something divine. This understanding forms the bedrock of our exploration into the genesis of the soul, its purpose, and its profound relationship with the cosmos.

To speak of a "divine blueprint" is not to suggest a literal, architectural plan, etched in celestial stone. Instead, the term is meant to invoke the image of a preordained design, a fundamental architecture inherent in the very fabric of existence and subtly woven into the tapestry of creation. This blueprint, if we may use the metaphor, encapsulates the essence of what it means to be human. It encompasses our inherent capacities, tendencies, and potential, and speaks of the unique purpose each soul is intended to fulfill. It addresses the purpose of every individual that unfolds throughout the course of a lifetime.

Consider, for instance, the ancient Greek concept of daimon, a personal spirit or guiding principle often associated with individual destiny. Plato, in his dialogues, explores the notion of the soul as possessing innate knowledge, a pre-existing wisdom that emerges as we progress through life. This intrinsic knowledge, he argues, reflects the soul's prior existence in the realm of forms—a realm of perfect ideals and archetypes. It echoes certain theological traditions, in which the soul originates from a pre-existent state before its union with the physical body.

The Kabbalistic tradition within Judaism offers a fascinating perspective on the creation of the soul. Kabbalah posits that souls are emanations of the Divine, sparks of the Ein Sof, the boundless and infinite God. These sparks, prior to their embodiment, exist in a state of potential, where they wait to be individualized and manifested in the physical world. The journey of the soul, therefore, reveals its inherent divinity, bringing forth its unique contribution to the cosmic harmony. The process of embodiment is seen not as a fall from grace, but rather as a necessary stage in the soul's evolution.

Christianity, in its varied interpretations, also offers compelling perspectives. Some theological streams suggest that the soul is created at the moment of conception, already imbued with a divine spark. At that stage, it has capacity for love, compassion, and communion with God.

Others envision a more complex relationship, where the soul's creation involves a collaboration between divine agency and human participation. Augustine, for instance, grappled with the problem of the original sin. He recognized the inherent human capacity for both good and evil, and suggested a pre-existent capacity within the soul that is only marred by the fall. This inherent duality, essentially the potential for both spiritual ascent and descent, reflects the intrinsic complexities of the divine blueprint itself.

Similarly, Islam addresses the creation of the soul in its theological texts. The Quran speaks of the soul (ruh) as being breathed into the human body by God. This position underlines the soul's divine origin, and its vital role in human existence. The human soul is considered a sacred trust, responsible for navigating life's trials and fulfilling its purpose according to God's will. The Islamic concept of qadr or predestination emphasizes the divine plan within which each soul plays a specific role. However, free will is also a central element, which highlights the human capacity to make choices within the context of this divine design.

The concept of a divine blueprint is not confined to frameworks that are explicitly religious.

Philosophical approaches also engage in the idea of inherent human potential. Existentialist thinkers, for example, while often emphasizing individual freedom and responsibility, acknowledge the profound influence our inherent nature has on our choices and actions. Although they reject the notion of a pre-ordained plan, they recognize the existence of an underlying structure within the human existence—an inherent drive for meaning, purpose, and authenticity.

Therefore, for us to understand our life's purpose, it is imperative that we understand our inherent nature. This understanding requires careful reflection on our strengths, weaknesses, tendencies, and inclinations. What are our natural aptitudes? What are our deepest passions and desires? What seems to come to us naturally; almost effortlessly? These clues can help us decipher the whispers of our inner selves, those gentle prompts that guide us towards the fulfillment of our unique purpose.

This journey of self-discovery is not always easy. Obstacles and challenges inevitably arise, testing our resolve and forcing us to confront our limitations. Yet, it is through these experiences that we learn, grow, and become more fully aware of ourselves. Reverting to the metaphor, the divine blueprint is not a static plan. Rather, it is a dynamic framework that allows for adaptation, growth, and transformation.

Furthermore, the concept of a divine blueprint challenges us to reconsider our understanding of "success." Often, we equate success to material wealth, social status, or personal achievement.

However, from the theological and philosophical perspectives, true success lies in the fulfillment of our inherent purpose, which embodies living a life aligned with our deepest values and aspirations. While this may not always translate into conventional measures of success, it resonates deeply within the soul, giving fulfillment that transcends any worldly accolades.

The divine blueprint is not a rigid formula meant to dictate every aspect of our lives. It is a guiding principle, an underlying architecture that helps to shape our potential. It is a framework that encourages exploration and allows for individual expression and creativity within the larger design. It is the subtle hum of possibilities, the inherent drive that pushes us to realize our potential and become the best versions of ourselves. Understanding this inherent nature or divine blueprint is the first step toward living a truly purposeful and fulfilling life.

This understanding is not solely the province of the devout; it is more comprehensive. It speaks to the fundamental human quest for meaning and purpose; a quest that resonates regardless of religious belief or philosophical perspective. The exploration of this inherent nature is a lifelong journey, a continual process of self-discovery and unfolding. It is a journey guided by the subtle prompts of our inner selves and informed by the diverse wisdom of human experience.

The Souls Journey Before Birth:
A Pre-existential State

The exploration of the soul's genesis naturally leads to a contemplation of its state before birth. Did it exist in some form, waiting for its earthly embodiment? This question has fueled millennia of theological debate and philosophical inquiry, giving rise to a rich tapestry of beliefs and interpretations. The concept of a pre-existential state for the soul challenges our conventional understanding of life's beginning, prompting us to consider the possibility of a journey that stretches far beyond the confines of our physical existence.

One of the most prominent perspectives of the soul's pre-birth state is found in the various doctrines of reincarnation. Many Eastern religions, including Hinduism, Buddhism, Jainism, and Sikhism, embrace the cyclical nature of existence. They posit that the soul transmigrates from one life to another, evolving through a series of births and rebirths, accumulating karma in the process. This cyclical journey is not merely a repetition but a process of spiritual growth and transformation. The soul, in this view, carries the accumulated experiences and lessons learned from past lives, which in turn help to shape its character and influence its trajectory in subsequent incarnations. The selection of a new life, the type of body it gets to inhabit, and the circumstances of the eventual birth, are all seen as consequences of the soul's karma and evolutionary trajectory. Detailed accounts of past lives, often recounted through hypnotic regression or spontaneous recollections, add another layer of intrigue to these beliefs. While scientifically unverifiable, these narratives offer compelling evidence albeit at a subjective level, on the reality of

reincarnation.

Furthermore, within this framework, the idea of a "soul's blueprint" takes on new meaning. Instead of a static plan determined solely at the moment of creation, it becomes a dynamic record of the soul's progression across lifetimes. Each life serves as a learning experience, refining and shaping the soul's essence, much like a sculptor meticulously chiseling away at a block of marble to reveal the figure within. This notion of continuous refinement challenges the linear progression model often associated with Western thought.

It suggests a cyclical, iterative process of growth and evolution. The pre-birth state, therefore, is not simply a waiting period, but rather a phase of preparation for the next chapter in the soul's grand narrative.

Beyond reincarnation, other belief systems posit a pre-existential state for the soul, which does not necessarily subscribe to the concept of cyclical rebirth. Platonism, for instance, suggests that the soul already exists before its union with the body, and possesses innate knowledge and memory of its pre-existent state even when it enters the realm of Forms. This pre-existent state is not a stage of physical existence, but rather a realm of pure ideas and archetypes—a realm of perfect beauty, justice, and truth. The soul, according to Plato, is gradually re-acquainted with this innate knowledge throughout its earthly existence.

This process, known as anamnesis or recollection, involves bringing to conscious awareness the inherent wisdom the soul already possesses. The journey of the soul, therefore, becomes a process of remembering and rediscovering its inherent connection to the realm of Form, which is its true home.

The Kabbalistic tradition in Judaism, as previously touched upon, offers a compelling vision of the soul's pre-embodiment state.

Kabbalistic teachings describe souls as sparks of the Ein Sof that emanate from the divine source. These sparks, prior to their manifestation in the physical world, exist in a state of potential, awaiting their moment of individualization. Each soul possesses a unique purpose, a specific role within the larger cosmic drama. The embodiment of the soul is thus not a descent but rather a deployment—it ventures forth from the divine into the material world to fulfill a unique purpose. The journey of the soul becomes one of expressing its inherent divinity while fulfilling its role within the grand tapestry of existence.

Similar concepts appear in various Christian theological streams, though with different interpretations. Some theologians emphasize the creation of the soul at the moment of conception, endowing it with a divine spark or inherent capacity for love and communion with God. However, other traditions posit a more nuanced perspective, suggesting a pre-existent state, perhaps in a heavenly realm. Augustine's writings, for example, grapple with the problem of the original sin, implying an innate capacity for both good and evil that pre-dates the soul's earthly existence. This inherent duality reflects the complexity of the human condition, and the perpetual struggle everyone experiences, between light and darkness.

As explained in the concept of the Divine Blueprint, the concept of the soul (ruh) within the Islamic theology is central. The Quran describes God breathing the ruh into the human body, emphasizing its divine origin and vital role in human life. The human soul is regarded as a sacred trust, responsible for fulfilling its purpose in accordance with God's will. While the concept of predestination (qadar) highlights the divine plan within which each soul has a specific role, the emphasis on free will recognizes humanity's capacity for choice and action.

The pre-birth state of the soul within Islamic thought remains a subject of interpretation and contemplation, but its inherent divine nature is undeniable.

Beyond theological and religious perspectives, philosophical

inquiries have explored the possibility of a pre-existential state for the soul or consciousness. Some philosophers have suggested the possibility of the consciousness being a fundamental aspect of the universe, which exists independently of the physical brain. The idea of universal consciousness, a collective field of awareness, suggests that individual souls or consciousnesses might exist within this larger field prior to their manifestation in different physical bodies. This concept echoes certain mystical traditions that speak of a unified consciousness or a divine ground from which all individual souls emerge.

Further, the very nature of time and space becomes a crucial consideration. If we accept the possibility of realms beyond our current understanding of space and time, then the concept of a pre-birth state for the soul becomes significantly more plausible.

Concepts like the multiverse, string theory, and quantum physics, blur the lines between what we perceive as reality, and the possibility of other dimensions or planes of existence. These scientific concepts, while not directly proving the existence of a pre-birth state, certainly open the door to considering that possibility.

In conclusion, the question of the soul's journey before birth is complex and multifaceted, and engages diverse religious, philosophical and scientific perspectives. While definitive proof remains elusive, the exploration of this question continues to enrich our understanding of the human condition, and our place within the cosmos. Whether we embrace the cyclical journeys of reincarnation, the pre-existent knowledge of Platonism, the divine emanations of Kabbalah, the creation narratives of various religious traditions, or the speculative concepts of modern physics, the notion of a soul's pre-birth state compels us to consider the vast and mysterious tapestry of existence and the profound journey of the human soul.

The soul's pre-birth state remains a powerful metaphor that highlights the inherent mysteries of existence and reminds us that our lives may be part of a much larger and more expansive narrative than we initially thought. The exploration of this mystery continues to inspire and challenge us, leading us towards a deeper understanding of ourselves and our relationship with the Divine. This holds true irrespective of how we define this mystery.

Embodiment and the Human Experience: The Souls Arrival

The journey of the soul extends far beyond the confines of our earthly existence. Nevertheless, the pivotal moment, signified by the dramatic shift from the ethereal to the tangible, occurs at birth. This is not merely a biological event. It is a profound spiritual transition, marked by a convergence of the seen and unseen, the divine and the material. The arrival of the soul into the body is a mystery that has captivated theologians, philosophers, and mystics for centuries. How does a pre-existing entity, existing perhaps in a realm beyond our comprehension, become inextricably bound to a physical form?

This union of soul and body is frequently described using metaphors that emphasize the integration of two seemingly disparate entities.

The body, which serves as the vessel, provides the framework for experience, the conduit through which the soul interacts with the physical world.

The soul, which is the animating principle, breathes life into the body, bestowing upon its consciousness, sentience, and the capacity for love, joy, sorrow, and all the complex emotions that define human experience. Some traditions liken this relationship to that of a pilot and an aircraft, where the soul is the pilot and the body the aircraft. Hence, it is the soul guiding the body through the journey of life. Others speak of the body as a garment, a temporary dwelling for the soul. Regardless of the specific metaphor used, the central idea remains: the soul is not merely a segment of the body, but its essence. It is the characteristic that defines the body.

However, this union is not always seamless. The transition from a pre-existent state to embodied existence can be fraught with challenges and potential conflicts. The process of adapting to the constraints of physicality can be jarring, as the soul adjusts to the limitations of a material world. The immediacy of sensory experience, the pull of desires and appetites, the vulnerability to pain and suffering, all contrast sharply with the presumed tranquility of a pre-existent state. This inherent tension between the ethereal nature of the soul and the material nature of the body forms a recurring theme in many spiritual traditions. It is a source of both struggle and growth, a crucible in which the soul is refined and shaped.

The challenges faced at birth extend beyond the mere adjustment to physicality. The circumstances of birth, the environment into which the soul is born, the cultural and familial influences all play a significant role in shaping the individual's spiritual trajectory. A soul born into a nurturing environment, surrounded by love and support, might have a smoother transition and a more positive outlook to life, than a soul born into hardship and depravation.

However, even within challenging circumstances, the inherent resilience of the soul shines through, demonstrating its capacity to navigate adversity and find meaning amidst suffering.

Moreover, the integration of the soul into the body is not a passive process. It requires active participation, a conscious engagement with the world and with one's own inner experience. The soul must learn to navigate the complex labyrinth of emotions, desires, and impulses, which characterize human life. It must confront the challenges associated with self-discovery and understanding of its own strengths and weaknesses, as well as those that come up when trying to find its place in the world. This is a lifelong journey, a constant process of learning, growing, and evolving.

The act of birth itself extends beyond the physical process; it also holds profound spiritual significance. In many cultures, it is considered a sacred event and is marked by rituals and ceremonies aimed at welcoming the new soul into the world. It is a celebration meant to bless the soul's journey. These rituals, whether religious or secular, often reflect the belief that the entry of a soul into the world is not a random occurrence, but rather a purposeful act within a larger cosmic plan.

In some theological perspectives, birth is seen as a moment of divine intervention, a deliberate act of creation. The soul, a spark of the Divine, is bestowed upon the body, initiating a unique and irreplaceable life. This perspective emphasizes the sacredness of human life and the inherent worth of every individual. The soul, infused with the Divine, possesses an innate capacity for goodness, love, and communion with God. The journey of life, then, becomes a quest for self-realization, a pursuit to fulfill the divine purpose for which each soul was created.

However, other perspectives acknowledge a potential conflict between the divine purpose and the human will. The inherent freedom of choice, the capacity for both good and evil, can lead to a divergence between the intended spiritual trajectory and the actual lived experience. This conflict often lies at the heart of human drama, prompting individuals to grapple with ethical dilemmas, moral choices, and consequences of their actions. From this perspective, the journey of the soul is not a predetermined path but a dynamic interplay between divine intention and human agency.

The interplay between the soul and the body as experienced through the birth lens, also underscores the interconnectedness of the individual with the cosmos. The soul, before birth, is not isolated; it exists within a larger web of existence, a spiritual realm that connects all living things. Birth, therefore, is not simply an entry into the physical world, but also a re-connection to this larger web. It embodies the process of reintegration into the cosmic dance of life. Understanding this reality underlines the responsibility we have as human beings, to nurture and preserve the integrity of this web. This means it is imperative that we respect the interconnectedness of all beings.

Ultimately, the arrival of the soul into the physical world at birth marks a pivotal transition. It is a moment of both wonder and challenge, a union of the ethereal and the material. It is the moment when the Divine and the human merge. The complexities of this union continue to inspire spiritual exploration, and to foster a profound sense of awe and wonder. The mystery of existence itself is a marvel, just as is our place within the larger cosmic narrative. The challenges faced as the soul transitions into the physical world shape its character and compels it to navigate the complexities of human experience. They also drive it to forge its unique path towards fulfillment.

The study of this pivotal moment, therefore, remains a vital cornerstone in understanding the essence of what it means to be human, and of our ongoing relationship with the Divine. The perpetual exploration of this theme continues to deepen our understanding of life and death, and of the mysteries that lie beyond.

The Unveiling of Purpose: Discovering Our Role in the Cosmic Order

The profound mystery of the soul's entry into the physical world at birth naturally leads to a compelling question: What is the purpose of this journey? What role does each individual soul play within the grand cosmic drama unfolding around us? This inquiry has driven countless individuals throughout history – philosophers, theologians, mystics, and ordinary people– on quests for meaning and fulfillment. However, there is no simple answer. The answer resides within the nexus of the individual's free will, and a larger, often unseen, divine plan.

Some theological traditions posit a preordained purpose for each soul. This perspective suggests that before entering the physical realm, each soul possesses an inherent nature with a unique set of talents, and a specific role to play within the greater cosmic order.

This "divine blueprint," as some might call it, is not necessarily revealed immediately upon birth, but rather unfolds gradually throughout life as the individual encounters challenges and opportunities that shape their character and purpose. The journey then becomes a process of self-discovery, a quest to uncover and fulfill the divinely ordained destiny.

Consider, for instance, the concept of "calling" in various religious and spiritual traditions. This notion suggests divine summons to a particular vocation or life path, often felt as an irresistible pull towards a specific kind of service or contribution to the world. This call may manifest in various forms, starting from a passionate pursuit of artistic expression to a deep commitment to social justice or scientific discovery. The pursuit of this calling, then, becomes the primary expression of one's preordained purpose.

However, this view does not necessarily imply a deterministic fate.

The divine blueprint, if it exists, is not rigid or unyielding. It leaves room for the individual's free will, which influences how one chooses to respond to their calling and the challenges associated with it.

The individual's choices, actions, and decisions influence how their life's purpose unfolds, and creates a dynamic interplay between divine intention and human agency. Even within the framework of a preordained purpose, the path taken is seldom linear or predictable. Obstacles, setbacks, and unexpected opportunities continually present themselves along the way, and they end up shaping the journey the individual ultimately takes. They have the effect of deepening the individual's understanding of their role within the greater scheme of things.

Different religious and philosophical perspectives offer various models for understanding this divine purpose. In some traditions, the purpose is framed as service to a higher power or deity. Life becomes a sacred duty, an attempt to align one's will with the divine will. In others, the emphasis is on self-realization, a journey towards a state of spiritual enlightenment or union with the Divine. Still for others, emphasis is put on the importance of uplifting other people, fostering compassion, and promoting harmony within the community. Each tradition provides its own unique lens through which to interpret the purpose of life, but the common thread remains the connection between the individual and the larger cosmic reality.

The exploration of purpose also encompasses the question of suffering. Is there a divine explanation why suffering exists? Many traditions posit that suffering, while painful, is necessary. They view it as often serving a purpose in one's journey towards self-discovery and spiritual growth.

Essentially, therefore, challenges and adversity can lead to deeper self-awareness, greater empathy, and a strengthened sense of resilience. These trials can forge character, refine the soul, and reveal hidden strengths that might otherwise remain dormant. Furthermore, suffering can foster a deeper connection with others who have shared similar experiences, ultimately strengthening the bonds of compassion and sense of community for all involved.

Philosophical approaches offer alternative perspectives on purpose.

Existentialism, for instance, emphasizes individual freedom and responsibility, asserting that individuals create their own meaning and purpose through their choices and actions. There is no inherent cosmic plan, but rather a vast, open expanse of possibility in which each individual crafts their own unique journey. This perspective can be empowering, because it places the onus of identifying the meaning squarely on the individual. However, in the absence of a predetermined path, this perspective can also be daunting as it demands that the individual grapples with the responsibility of shaping their own life.

Humanism, in contrast, centers on human values and potential. Its focus is on the importance of human relationships, community, and the pursuit of knowledge and understanding. The pursuit of knowledge and self-improvement, along with contributions to the betterment of humanity, form the basis of a meaningful life. This perspective offers a secular framework for finding purpose, one that prioritizes human agency and collaboration in the pursuit of shared goals.

The quest for purpose is not a solitary undertaking. Throughout history, communities and religious institutions have played a significant role in helping individuals discover and fulfill their purpose. Social structures, traditions, and rituals often serve to guide individuals towards pursuing meaningful lives, where they contribute as they enjoy a sense of belonging and collective identity. The support of family, friends, and community can be crucial in navigating life's challenges, as it provides strength during moments of despair.

In conclusion, the unveiling of purpose is a lifelong journey of self-discovery, a quest to understand our role within the vast cosmic order. Whether guided by a preordained divine plan, or shaped by individual choices and experiences, the pursuit of meaning and fulfillment remains a fundamental aspect of human experience. The diverse perspectives offered by religious traditions and philosophical inquiries provide a rich tapestry of insights into this central question, reminding us of the complexity and beauty inherent in the journey of the soul.

Ultimately, it is through reflection, self-awareness, engagement with the world, and the support of others that we uncover the unique purpose each of us carries within our hearts; how we contribute to the ever-evolving narrative of the cosmos. The journey itself, with its challenges and triumphs, is as significant as the destination. This is because through the process of striving towards purpose we truly come to understand ourselves and our place within the universe. The search for our place in the cosmic tapestry is a continuous process of learning, growing, and evolving, a testament to the enduring human spirit and its inherent desire for meaning and connection. This ongoing quest, shared by countless individuals across time and cultures, underscores the profound mystery and enduring relevance of our existence.

The Devils Desire: A Misinterpretation of Connection

The conventional image of the devil, a malevolent entity actively seeking to claim human souls, often overshadows a more profound and nuanced truth. The devil's relentless pursuit, in theological terms, can be reinterpreted as a distorted reflection of the inherent longing for connection – a yearning deeply embedded within the human spirit, albeit misdirected. This yearning, in its purest form, represents our innate desire to connect with the Divine, a desire that fuels our spiritual quests and shapes our understanding of purpose.

The devil, in this reframed narrative, becomes a symbol of the seductive power of misdirected longing, a twisted mirror reflecting the human soul's desperate search for meaning, fulfillment, and ultimately, connection.

This perspective challenges the simplistic binary of good versus evil, offering instead a more complex understanding of spiritual dynamics. The devil's "desire" is not simply a malevolent grasping for power, but rather a perversion of the inherent human drive to connect – a corrupted echo of the soul's innate longing for communion with something larger than itself. This reinterpretation acknowledges the subtle and often insidious ways in which spiritual yearning can be manipulated and distorted, leading individuals down paths that ultimately separate them from the Divine rather than uniting them.

Consider the various temptations detailed in religious texts. These are not merely external forces, but internal struggles, reflecting the inner turmoil that arises when our deepest desires are channeled into self-serving pursuits rather than selfless service. The lure of power, wealth, and sensual pleasure often attributed to the devil's influence, are not inherently evil, but become so when they become the primary focus of our lives; when they eclipse our spiritual aspirations that serve our connection to something greater.

The devil's methods are characterized by deception and manipulation, exploiting the human vulnerabilities that arise from our inherent desires for belonging, acceptance, and significance. He appeals to our pride, our ambition, and our insecurities, twisting our innate yearning for connection into a pursuit of self-aggrandizement and dominance. This is precisely why the battle against "evil" is not simply an external conflict but an internal struggle, a constant negotiation between our higher aspirations and our baser instincts.

This internal conflict reflects the tension between our capacity for both profound love and devastating cruelty. The human spirit, capable of sublime acts of compassion and selfless devotion, is also capable of unspeakable acts of violence and destruction. The devil, in this context, does not represent an external antagonist, but an embodiment of the shadow self; the darker aspects of human nature that we must confront and integrate if we are to achieve spiritual wholeness.

Furthermore, the concept of the "fallen angel" adds another layer of complexity to this interpretation. If the devil was once a being of immense spiritual power and proximity to the Divine, his fall can be seen as a profound tragedy – a tragic misdirection of immense potential. This narrative suggests that even beings of immense spiritual power are not immune to the pitfalls of misdirected longing. It highlights the universal nature of the human struggle against temptation, and the ever-present possibility of falling from grace. The devil's story then becomes a cautionary tale, a reminder of the fragility of the spiritual connection. It also underlines the importance of remaining vigilant in our pursuit of the Divine.

The image of the devil frequently involves acts of deception and trickery, further highlighting the crucial role of discernment in our spiritual journey. The ability to distinguish between genuine connection and its deceptive counterfeits is paramount. This requires self-awareness, introspection, and a commitment to cultivating a critical consciousness. We must cultivate the capacity to question our motivations, examine our desires, and discern between authentic spiritual experiences and the delusive – those that ultimately lead us away from the Divine.

The theological concept of "spiritual warfare" can be reinterpreted through this lens. It is not a battle against an external enemy but an internal struggle for the soul's allegiance, a constant negotiation between the pull towards genuine connection and the allure of counterfeit substitutes. This internal battle necessitates constant self-examination, a willingness to confront our shadows, and a commitment to cultivating virtues that foster genuine connection with the Divine.

The consequences of succumbing to the devil's "desire," within this framework, are not simply eternal damnation, but a profound disconnection from the source of meaning and purpose. This disconnection manifests in various forms, ranging from feelings of emptiness and alienation to self-destructive behaviors and perpetual suffering. The "lost soul," therefore, is not simply a victim of malevolent forces, but an individual who has lost their way; one misdirected in their pursuit of genuine connection.

However, this interpretation offers a message of hope. The inherent human longing for connection, when properly channeled, can lead to a profound and transformative union with the Divine. The journey of the soul, then, becomes a process of aligning our desires with our spiritual aspirations; one that cultivates virtues that foster connection. Ultimately, this process helps us overcome the internal obstacles that prevent us from achieving true fulfillment.

The path to genuine connection is rarely easy. It requires effort, discipline, and a commitment to self-improvement. It involves confronting our shadows, acknowledging our vulnerabilities, and cultivating inner strength. But the rewards are monumental and immeasurable. Those who reap them lead a life of meaning, purpose, and lasting fulfillment. The ultimate victory over the "devil's desire" is not a triumph over an external enemy, but an internal transformation, a re-alignment of the human heart towards authentic connection with the Divine.

In conclusion, reinterpreting the devil's desire as a distorted reflection of humanity's yearning for connection unveils a deeper understanding of the spiritual journey. It moves beyond a simplistic good-versus-evil dichotomy, to embrace the complexity of the human spirit. This interpretation acknowledges the potential for both profound love and devastating self-destruction. The battle is not solely against an external force, but also one within – one represented by the constant internal struggle for alignment. Internally, there is always a quest for authentic connection, and it requires self-awareness, discernment, and a commitment to cultivating virtues that foster genuine communion with the Divine. The ultimate victory lies, not in conquering an external enemy, but in transforming the inner landscape of the soul.

The devil's distorted desire, thus, serves as a powerful metaphor that reflects the critical importance of discerning genuine connection and its seductive, yet ultimately empty, counterfeits. Such discernment serves as a constant reminder of the delicate balance between light and shadow within the human heart. The journey towards authentic connection is a life-long process of self-discovery, a pilgrimage of the soul towards its true home. It is a testament to the enduring human yearning for meaning and belonging.

The Tension Between Duty and Desire: Internal Conflicts

The human condition is a tapestry woven with threads of duty and desire, often intertwined in a complex and sometimes agonizing embrace. We are creatures of both profound responsibility and intense longing, and the friction between these two powerful forces shapes our lives in profound ways. This internal conflict, essentially the tension between what we ought to do and what we want to do, is a recurring theme throughout human history. It echoes in the lives of saints and sinners alike. It is a struggle played out not just on grand stages of historical significance, but within the quiet chambers of individual hearts.

Consider the historical figure of Abraham, as depicted in the Abrahamic faiths. Summoned by God to sacrifice his beloved son, Isaac, Abraham confronts a profound moral dilemma. His unwavering faith, with his sense of duty to God, is pitted against his deepest paternal instincts - his overwhelming love for his child. This is not a mere theoretical exercise, but a visceral, agonizing internal conflict that challenges the very foundations of his being. The narrative does not shy away from Abraham's emotional turmoil, the internal struggle between obedience and the primal urge to protect his son.

The very act of preparing for the sacrifice, which includes binding Isaac, underscores the immense internal conflict he experiences. There is an agonizing tension between divine command and human emotion. Abraham's eventual obedience, marked by his willingness to sacrifice what he held most dear, is not presented as a simple act of blind faith. On the contrary, it is a testament to the profound internal struggle he endures, a wrestling match between his duty to the Divine and his deepest desires. The story's enduring power lies not in the straightforward acceptance of divine authority, but in the raw human drama occasioned by the internal conflict.

This tension between duty and desire finds resonance in countless literary works. Sophocles' Antigone offers a compelling example. Antigone, faced with the laws of the state and moral duty to her family, chooses to bury her brother, effectively defying Creon's decree. This act, born of profound familial love and a sense of religious obligation, sets her on a collision course with the state, culminating in her tragic demise. Her story is a powerful exploration of the internal conflict between civic duty and personal morality. This conflict ultimately leads to her destruction. Antigone's unwavering commitment to her family's honor and religious beliefs illustrates the power of deeply held convictions, and the internal struggle between personal belief and state authority. This commitment persists despite the potential of fatal consequences and highlights the profound internal conflicts that can arise when moral duty clashes with the demands of society.

The internal conflict between duty and desire is not limited to grand narratives or historical figures; it is the daily experience for countless individuals. The conscientious objector who refuses military service based on deeply held moral principles embodies this tension. Their commitment to the convictions they hold often comes at a significant personal cost, which may include a sacrifice of societal acceptance, career advancement, or even personal safety. The inner struggle is not simply a rejection of authority, but a complex negotiation between their sense of duty to a higher power or moral code, and the societal pressures and expectations they face. Their choice is a testament to the power of internal convictions. It is a profound illustration of the human capacity to prioritize conscience over conformity.

Similarly, the doctor who chooses to serve in a resource-scarce environment faces personal hardship and limited resources; an act driven by a sense of duty. That doctor's commitment to alleviating suffering transcends personal gain. The decision to forgo a comfortable life to confront challenges and adversity requires profound commitment, essentially prioritization of the higher calling over personal ambitions. This scenario reflects the inner struggle between personal desire and commitment to greater good. That struggle remains a constant negotiation between personal fulfillment and service to others.

The complexities of this internal conflict are further amplified when duty and desire appear to be at odds with each other. Consider the individual torn between family responsibility and personal aspirations. The artists yearning for creative expression might grapple with the demands of providing for their family; finding themselves caught in constant negotiation between their artistic calling and familial obligations. The tension is not merely about time management. There is a deeper internal struggle, a balancing act between personal fulfillment and the moral imperative of family care.

Parents sometimes experience this tension acutely, as they wrestle with the demands of work and family life. The desire to provide for their family often clashes with the longing to be more present in their children's lives. This is not a question of prioritizing one over the other, but of constantly negotiating, adapting, and striving for a balance that may never fully materialize. The experience is profoundly human and highlights the complex and frequently conflicting desires that shape our lives.

Moreover, the notion of duty itself is multifaceted. Duty is not solely defined by external obligations; it is shaped by personal values, moral beliefs, and spiritual convictions. An individual's sense of duty may stem from their religious faith, their commitment to a social cause, or their deeply held personal ethics. This internal compass or personal sense of duty is a powerful force that can guide individuals' decisions and actions, often pushing them to act against their immediate desires or self-interest.

The internal conflict between duty and desire is not necessarily a negative experience. In fact, grappling with such tension can lead to profound personal growth and self-discovery. The act of wrestling with competing values, of confronting the conflict between what we want and what we believe to be right, can lead to a deeper understanding of ourselves and our priorities. It can illuminate our values, refine our understanding of personal moral compass, and shape our sense of purpose. It is in these struggles marked by moments of internal conflict that we discover the depth and complexity of the human spirit.

The journey is not about eliminating the tension, but rather, navigating through it. It is about understanding the intricacies of such tension, and, in the process, finding a path that integrates our duties and desires into a life of meaning and purpose.

The exploration of this internal conflict is not merely an intellectual exercise but also a journey into the heart of human experience. It is about understanding the forces that shape our lives, the internal struggles that define our choices, and the path that leads to a life that honors both our duties and our desires. The tension between these two powerful forces is not a problem to be solved, but a dynamic to be navigated. It is a journey of self-discovery that continues throughout our lives. For it is in the constant negotiation and the continual process of balancing competing values and aspirations that we come to a deeper understanding of what it truly means to be human.

This ongoing dialogue between duty and desire is the crucible in which character is forged, and from which a life of genuine meaning can emerge. It is the very essence of the human condition, a testament to our complexity. It represents our capacity for both selflessness and self-interest, as well as our enduring quest for meaning and purpose in a world filled with conflicting demands.

The Weight of Responsibility: Shouldering Our Burdens

The exploration of duty and desire naturally leads us to the weighty consideration of responsibility. We are not simply passive recipients of experiences tossed about by the currents of fate. Rather, we are active participants in the shaping of our lives. We are the authors of our own narratives, each choice being a brushstroke on the canvas of our existence. This agency, or capacity to act and to choose, brings with it a profound weight: the weight of responsibility.

This responsibility is multifaceted, as it encompasses both personal accountability and interconnectedness within society. On a personal level, responsibility involves acknowledging the consequences of our actions, both intended and unintended. The ripple effect of our choices, which extends far beyond our immediate sphere of influence, demands careful consideration. A seemingly insignificant decision can have profound and unforeseen repercussions, and this underscores the importance of mindful engagement with the world. This position is not meant to invoke a paralyzing fear of action, but rather to serve as a call to conscious decision-making. It is meant to prompt a commitment to understanding the potential ramifications of our choices before we act.

Consider, for instance, the ethical dilemmas faced by professionals in fields like medicine and law. A doctor, faced with a patient's critical condition and limited resources, must weigh the potential benefits and risks of different treatment options. This is not merely a clinical calculation. It is a moral decision where the doctor weighs probabilities against potential consequences of great magnitude. The surgeon's scalpel, the lawyer's arguments, and such other work tools are not just instruments of the respective professions. They are instruments of influence, capable of shaping lives and destinies. Their responsibility lies not only in their technical proficiency, but also in the ethical framework that guides their practice.

Similarly, the decisions of business leaders have far-reaching consequences, impacting not only their shareholders and employees but also the wider community and the environment. The pursuit of profit, while legitimate, must be tempered by a sense of social responsibility; a recognition of the ethical implications of business practices. Exploitation of labor, environmental degradation, and the prioritization of short-term gains over long-term sustainability, all reflect a failure to shoulder the weight of responsibility. A responsible business leader understands that success should be measured not only by financial metrics, but also by the positive impact their actions have on society and the environment.

Moving beyond the professional sphere, consider the everyday choices we make. A seemingly simple act, such as littering, contributes to a larger problem of environmental degradation. A casual online comment that lacks empathy or consideration can contribute to a climate of negativity and division. These seemingly minor actions, when multiplied across the population, have a cumulative impact that cannot be ignored. Our responsibility extends to the creation of a society that is just, sustainable, and compassionate. It requires a conscious effort to consider the collective consequences of individual actions, and hence to act responsibly; not just for us but for others.

The weight of responsibility extends beyond the realm of tangible actions, to encompass the cultivation of our inner lives. Spiritual growth is not a passive process but rather one of active engagement. It demands a conscious effort to cultivate virtues such as compassion, empathy, and self-awareness.

The spiritual journey involves taking responsibility for our thoughts, emotions, and behaviors, and recognizing the impact these have on ourselves and those around us.

We, therefore, must confront difficult aspects of ourselves, acknowledge our flaws, and strive to become better versions of ourselves. This is an ongoing process that demands constant self-reflection and a commitment to personal growth.

This responsibility for, or commitment to, our spiritual well-being is intimately connected to our social responsibility. Our relationship with others is not reflected in isolated occurrences but is deeply intertwined with our personal growth and spiritual development. The way we treat others, and the level of empathy and compassion we extend to them, reflects our own spiritual development. Responsibility, in this context, involves not only striving for personal growth, but also the fostering of positive relationships based on mutual respect, understanding, and empathy.

The idea of destiny, often viewed as predetermined, takes on a new dimension when viewed through the lens of responsibility. We are not merely passive recipients of fate but active participants in shaping our own destinies. Our choices, our actions, our commitment to personal and social responsibility all contribute to the trajectory of our lives. This does not imply that we can control every aspect of our destiny; it only underlines our role as agents, in navigating the challenges and opportunities that come our way.

However, this understanding of responsibility is not without challenges. The weight of our actions and the potential for negative consequences can be overwhelming. The sense of responsibility can lead to feelings of guilt, inadequacy, and even despair. This is particularly true in situations where our actions have unintended negative consequences; situations where we feel powerless to undo the harm we have caused.

Navigating these feelings requires a nuanced approach. While it is essential that we acknowledge our mistakes and take responsibility for our actions, this should not be equated with self-flagellation. Learning from our mistakes, making amends where possible, and focusing on future positive actions is a crucial part of the process. To navigate the weight of responsibility, it is necessary that we have self-compassion, an understanding of our own limitations, and a commitment to continuous growth. As the concept of collective responsibility also deserves consideration. Often, the negative consequences of our actions are not felt solely by us, but also by the wider community. Environmental degradation, social injustice, and economic inequality are all examples of challenges that require collective action: a shared sense of responsibility. Addressing these problems demands collaboration, empathy, and a willingness to work together. This way, we can create a more just and sustainable world, as we recognize that our actions are intertwined and that our responsibility extends beyond our individual spheres of influence.

Granted the weight of responsibility is demanding, but it is not a burden to be avoided. It is an essential element of human experience, a catalyst for growth and a source of meaning and purpose.

Besides, it is not only morally imperative that we embrace this responsibility, acknowledge the consequences of our actions, and strive to live a life guided by ethical principles, but it is also deeply fulfilling. It is in the mindful acceptance of our role in the world that we find true freedom; a freedom that comes not from escaping the weight of our responsibilities, but from actively engaging with them.

It is in this engagement that we find a path toward a life of authenticity, purpose, and lasting fulfillment. The very act of shouldering our burdens, confronting the complexities of our choices and their consequences, is what truly defines our journey as human beings. And it is on this journey, with all its challenges and rewards, that we discover the profound depth and richness of the human spirit.

The Pursuit of Happiness vs The Fulfillment of Purpose

The previous discussion on responsibility laid the groundwork for understanding the crucial distinction between the pursuit of happiness and the fulfillment of purpose. While happiness is often sought as a primary goal, a life solely dedicated to pleasure often proves unsatisfying and ultimately ephemeral. True and lasting fulfillment, I posit, stems from a deeper source: the alignment of our lives with a divinely ordained purpose – alignment that gives a sense of meaning that transcends individual desires. This is not to diminish the importance of happiness, but rather to situate it within a larger framework of meaning and purpose. Happiness, in this context, becomes a byproduct, a natural consequence of living a life aligned with our inherent nature. It comes naturally as we play our role within a larger cosmic order.

Consider the diverse perspectives of various faith traditions. In Christianity, for example, the concept of "vocation" points towards a divinely appointed purpose. Individuals are called to specific roles and responsibilities, not necessarily for personal gain or pleasure, but for the purpose of serving God and fellow humans. This vocation may involve careers, family life, or acts of service, but they all contribute to a larger divine plan.

The pursuit of personal happiness, while not condemned, is seen as secondary to fulfilling this God-given purpose. A life lived in accordance with God's will, regardless of the immediate circumstances, is ultimately seen as a path to genuine fulfillment. This is true irrespective of any hardship or suffering borne. The beatitudes in the Sermon on the Mount, for instance, extol the virtues of those who are meek, merciful, and peacemakers—qualities not always associated with immediate happiness, but rather with a deeper spiritual fulfillment.

Islam, too, emphasizes the concept of purpose through the concept of taqwa, often translated as piety or God-consciousness. A life lived in accordance with Allah's will, as revealed in the Quran and the Sunnah (prophetic tradition), is deemed a life of purpose and ultimate fulfillment. This includes adherence to religious practices, ethical conduct, and social justice. The goal, the ultimate purpose, is to achieve jannah (paradise); a state of ultimate bliss and fulfillment achieved through obedience to God and righteous actions. The rewards are not solely material. They transcend into a spiritual realm, demonstrating that true fulfillment is not merely a fleeting sensation, but a lasting state achieved through adherence to a higher purpose.

Buddhism, while not centered around a personal God as in Christianity or Islam, still emphasizes the pursuit of enlightenment and the fulfillment of a spiritual purpose as the goal.

This involves overcoming suffering, achieving Nirvana, and ultimately escaping the cycle of rebirth. The Buddhist path, with its emphasis on meditation, mindfulness, and ethical conduct, is not primarily concerned with the pursuit of fleeting happiness. Instead, it is concerned mainly with the cultivation of wisdom, compassion, and spiritual growth. The eradication of suffering and the attainment of enlightenment represent the ultimate fulfillment, a state that transcends the ephemeral nature of worldly pleasures. The path itself, with its challenges and hardships, is seen as integral to the process of achieving this ultimate purpose.

Judaism, similarly, frames a life of purpose through the concept of mitzvot —divine commandments. These commandments are not simply rules to follow, but opportunities to participate in God's work in the world. Living a life according to the Torah, engaging in acts of charity, justice, and righteousness, is seen as fulfilling a divine purpose and contributing to the repair of the world (Tikkun Olam). This perspective highlights the fact that it is not inherently wrong to pursue happiness, but such pursuit should be balanced with a sense of responsibility as one contributes to the larger community and the divine plan. The emphasis is on participation within a larger narrative; contributing to something greater than oneself.

Comparing these traditions reveals a common thread: the concept of purpose as an integral part of a fulfilling life. While the specific nature of this purpose may vary depending on the faith or tradition, the underlying principle remains consistent: true and lasting fulfillment comes not from the relentless pursuit of happiness, but from living a life aligned with a higher purpose. This means contributing to something larger than oneself. The emphasis shifts from the desires of the individual to a sense of responsibility, and participation in a cosmic or divine plan.

This perspective challenges the modern Western concept, where emphasis on the individual's happiness is the goal. While the pursuit of happiness is certainly a legitimate desire, framing it as the only goal can lead to disillusionment and dissatisfaction. A life solely focused on pleasure, devoid of purpose and meaning, often fails to provide lasting fulfillment. The hedonistic pursuit of happiness, while having potential to yield fleeting moments of joy, often leaves a void; a sense of emptiness that no amount of material possessions or sensory pleasure can fill.

The pursuit of purpose, on the other hand, provides a framework for navigating life's complexities. When one knows their role and understands their place within a larger context, their life has a sense of direction and meaning. They no longer take challenges and hardships, inevitable aspects of human experience, as obstacles to happiness. but as opportunities for growth, learning, and spiritual development. This does not imply a life of stoic resignation or passive acceptance of suffering. Rather, it calls for an active engagement with life's challenges. It is a commitment to live a life of purpose, where one contributes to something greater than themselves.

This is not a call to abandon the pursuit of happiness, but rather a call for a re-evaluation of its place in our lives. Happiness, in this context, is not the goal but a byproduct, a natural consequence of living a life aligned with our purpose. It is a state of being that arises from a deeper sense of meaning and fulfillment, a sense of connection to something larger than us. True happiness, then, is not simply a feeling, but a state achieved through a life lived with purpose and intention. This understanding demands a shift in perspective. We must re-evaluate our priorities and values and commit to living a life that is not only personally fulfilling but also beneficial to the larger good.

The path to this deeper fulfillment is rarely straightforward. Often, it involves confronting difficult choices, navigating moral dilemmas, and enduring hardship. But it is in these struggles that we discover our true potential; our capacity for resilience and our ability to find meaning in the face of adversity. The journey itself, with its challenges and rewards, becomes an essential part of this process, whereby we discover our purpose and achieve true fulfillment. It is a journey of self-discovery, a process of continuous growth and transformation that leads to a more profound and lasting sense of meaning and purpose. It is one that transcends the boundaries of individual happiness, leading to a life of deeper fulfillment and lasting satisfaction. The commitment to this journey, or pursuit of purpose, is perhaps the most important commitment we can make.

The Path of Righteousness: Aligning Actions with Purpose

The previous exploration of purpose and fulfillment provides a crucial foundation for understanding the path of righteousness.

We have already established that a life aligned with a higher purpose, whether divinely ordained or self-discovered, leads to a more profound sense of fulfillment than one geared solely toward the pursuit of happiness. We now turn to the practical implications of the choices we make and the actions we take, this being the realm of ethics; the moral compass that guides us along this path. It is not enough to simply identify our purpose; we must actively strive to align our actions with it. This alignment is not passive acceptance but active engagement, a continuous striving toward moral excellence.

Virtue ethics provides a valuable framework for understanding this process. Unlike consequentialist ethics, which focuses on the outcomes of actions, or deontological ethics, which emphasizes adherence to rules and duties, virtue ethics centers on the character of the moral agent. It not only asks "What should I do?" but also "What kind of person should I be?" The path of righteousness, therefore, becomes a journey of cultivating virtuous character traits—honesty, compassion, justice, courage, temperance, and so forth. These virtues are not simply abstract ideals, but dispositions that shape our actions and guide our choices. They are habits of thought and action cultivated over time through conscious effort and reflection.

Consider the life of Mahatma Gandhi, a powerful example of the transformative power of virtuous living. Gandhi's commitment to nonviolent resistance, his unwavering adherence to truthfulness (Satya), and his dedication to social justice, fundamentally altered the political landscape of India and inspired movements for social change worldwide. His actions were not merely strategic moves to achieve political goals; they stemmed from deeply ingrained virtuous dispositions. His commitment to Ahimsa (non-violence) was not a mere tactic, but a profound moral principle that shaped his entire life. This principle, deeply rooted in his spiritual beliefs, guided his political strategy, his personal relationships, and his daily actions. His life is a testament to the power of virtuous living; how it can help achieve meaningful and lasting change.

Similarly, the life of Martin Luther King Jr. exemplifies the profound impact of virtuous actions on the path to social justice. Dr. King's unwavering commitment to nonviolent resistance in the face of immense oppression, his powerful articulation of the moral imperative for racial equality, and his unwavering dedication to love and forgiveness during hatred and violence, demonstrate the transformative power of virtuous character. His moral leadership inspired millions to join the struggle for civil rights, and fundamentally changed the course of American history.

Like Gandhi, Dr. King's actions were not merely tactical maneuvers; they flowed from a deeply rooted commitment to justice, compassion, and love. His unwavering commitment to these virtues shaped his every decision and ultimately led to profound and lasting social change.

However, the path of righteousness is not always smooth or easy. It often involves confronting difficult choices, navigating moral dilemmas, and enduring hardships. The virtuous person does not avoid challenges, but instead meets them with courage, integrity, and wisdom. This requires a constant process of self-reflection, moral deliberation, and a willingness to learn from mistakes. It involves recognizing our own limitations, acknowledging our biases, and actively striving to cultivate virtuous dispositions.

Consider the ethical dilemmas faced by individuals in positions of power. For instance, a leader may face the difficult choice between adhering to a principle and achieving a desired outcome. A politician may be tempted to compromise their integrity for the sake of political expediency, while a business leader may be pressured to prioritize profit over ethical considerations. Even a judge may face the difficult task of balancing justice with mercy. These situations call for careful moral deliberation, a willingness to prioritize ethical principles even when they are costly. They also require a commitment to act in accordance with one's conscience.

The choices we make, irrespective of their apparent magnitude or significance, accumulate over time to shape our character and define our lives. A single act of dishonesty, a moment of cruelty, or an act of injustice can erode our moral integrity, and undermine our ability to live a life aligned with our purpose. Conversely, consistent acts of kindness, compassion, justice, and courage strengthen our virtuous dispositions, and lead us closer to our ideal self. This accumulation of actions, particularly the conscious striving toward virtuous living, is what defines the path of righteousness.

Furthermore, this path often requires us to confront not only external challenges, but also our own internal struggles. Our ego, our desires, and our attachments, can often pull us away from the path of virtue. The path requires self-awareness, the ability to recognize our own shortcomings, and a willingness to engage in a process of self-improvement. Spiritual practices, such as meditation, prayer, or mindfulness, can be invaluable tools in this process.

These practices help us to cultivate self-awareness and inner peace and develop emotional regulation skills. The cultivation of inner peace is, in turn, essential for navigating the challenges of moral life, and for maintaining a steady commitment to the path of righteousness.

It is important to note that the path of righteousness is not a solitary journey. We are all interconnected and our actions have consequences that extend beyond ourselves. Our relationships with others, our participation in the community, and our contribution to the larger world are all integral parts of the path. The pursuit of righteousness is not just about personal virtue, but also about social responsibility and justice. This highlights the interdependence of individual and societal well-being. A life that is truly righteous involves a commitment to both personal moral excellence and social justice.

This interconnectedness underscores the importance of empathy and compassion in moral life. The ability to understand and share the feelings of others, to see ourselves in them, and act in ways that promote their well-being, is essential for navigating the complexities of ethical decision-making. The path of righteousness, therefore, is not simply a matter of following rules or adhering to principles; it is also a matter of cultivating empathy, compassion, and a commitment to social justice. The more we cultivate these virtues, the more we can act in ways that promote our own well-being as well as that of others. This creates a virtuous cycle, where our commitment to righteousness leads to a deeper sense of connection, purpose, and fulfillment.

Finally, the path of righteousness is a lifelong journey and not a destination. It requires continuous effort, self-reflection, and a commitment to growth and transformation. We will, inevitably, make mistakes, fall short of our ideals, and face challenges that test our resolve, but it is through these struggles, failures, and successes that we grow in wisdom, compassion, and moral character.

The journey itself, with its challenges and triumphs, becomes an integral part of the process of achieving true and lasting fulfillment. The unwavering commitment to this ongoing process — the continual striving towards moral excellence—is what truly defines the path of righteousness. The true measure of a life lived righteously is not the absence of mistakes, but the willingness to learn from them. It is the willingness to grow from them, and to continue striving toward a more virtuous and fulfilling life.

Challenges and Obstacles: Overcoming Adversity

The pursuit of a life aligned with our purpose, the path of righteousness, is rarely straightforward. It is paved not just with moments of clarity and triumph, but also with significant challenges, setbacks, and periods of profound suffering. These obstacles, far from being mere impediments, often serve as crucial catalysts for growth. They push us to develop resilience, deepen our understanding of ourselves and the world, and ultimately achieve a more profound sense of fulfillment. The very act of overcoming adversity often shapes our character in a more profound way, than periods of ease and comfort ever could.

Consider the experience of illness. The physical and emotional suffering associated with disease can force us to confront our mortality, re-evaluate our priorities, and appreciate the fragility of life. This forced introspection can lead to a deeper understanding of our own values and engineer a renewed appreciation for our relationships. It can also strengthen our commitment to living a life of meaning and purpose. Many individuals who have faced life-threatening illnesses report a profound shift in perspective. They report a newfound appreciation for the simple joys of life, and a renewed sense of purpose. The struggle itself becomes a transformative process, which helps to forge resilience and a deeper understanding of the human condition.

Similarly, experiences of loss, such as the death of a loved one, end of a significant relationship, or loss of a cherished possession, can be profoundly destabilizing. The grief and pain associated with such loss can challenge our sense of self, our beliefs about the world, and our faith in the future. However, once we navigate these difficult emotions, process the pain, and ultimately find a way to integrate the loss into our lives, the experience can lead to a significant deepening of our empathy, compassion, and wisdom. It is through confronting our vulnerability, acknowledging our grief, and allowing ourselves to feel the full range of human emotions that we manage to emerge stronger, more compassionate, and more attuned to the human experience.

Financial hardship, another significant obstacle on the path to fulfillment, can force us to confront our values, our priorities, and our relationship to material possessions. The stress and anxiety associated with financial insecurity can be overwhelming, but once we navigate these difficulties, we often discover unexpected strengths, resourcefulness, and a deeper appreciation for the importance of community and support. Overcoming financial challenges has the capacity to foster a greater sense of self-reliance, a stronger work ethic, and a renewed commitment to living within our means. It also deepens our empathy for others facing similar struggles.

Social injustice and oppression represent profound challenges that affect individuals as well as entire communities. The struggle for social justice and the fight against discrimination and inequality often demands tremendous courage, resilience, and unwavering commitment to ethical principles. These struggles can be arduous, demanding, and at times, deeply disheartening. Yet, it is through confronting such injustices and fighting for a more equitable world that we can find a deeper sense of meaning, purpose, and fulfillment. The very act of working towards a better world for others often leads to a profound transformation within oneself.

Overcoming adversity requires a combination of inner strength, resilience, and the ability to draw upon external support systems. It entails fostering strong relationships with family, friends, and the community, seeking professional help when needed, and engaging in self-care practices that promote physical and emotional well-being. By developing strong spiritual practice, which involves prayer, meditation, or engaging with nature, one experiences a sense of grounding, hope, and perspective, during difficult times. Spiritual practices help us cultivate inner resilience and enable us to navigate challenges with greater equanimity and inner strength.

Furthermore, the cultivation of a growth mindset is crucial in navigating the inevitable obstacles on the path to fulfillment. A growth mindset, as opposed to a fixed mindset, emphasizes the belief that our abilities and intelligence are not fixed traits, but rather capacities with potential to develop and improve through effort and learning. This perspective allows us to embrace challenges as opportunities for growth, learn from our mistakes, and view setbacks as steppingstones to progress rather than failures. This mindset is essential for building resilience and cultivating a sense of agency and control in the face of adversity.

Finally, it is important to remember that the path to fulfillment is not a linear progression. It is a journey characterized by both progress and setbacks, by moments of clarity and periods of confusion, and by triumphs and failures. Embracing the inevitable challenges and setbacks as integral parts of this journey allows us to cultivate greater self-awareness, resilience, and a deeper understanding of ourselves and our place in the world.

It is through confronting our limitations, acknowledging our vulnerabilities, and learning from our mistakes that we ultimately grow in wisdom and compassion, and develop a deeper appreciation for the preciousness of life. The challenges themselves, therefore, become essential elements in forging a well-lived life, a life of purpose and fulfillment, a life truly lived on the path of righteousness. The scars we bear from these battles are not signs of defeat but rather testaments to our resilience, strength, and unwavering commitment to the journey itself. The ultimate measure of a life well-lived is not the absence of suffering, but the courage, wisdom, and compassion with which we navigate it.

Defining Good and Evil: A Multifaceted Perspective

The seemingly straightforward concepts of "good" and "evil" unravel into a complex tapestry when examined through the lens of diverse cultures and religious traditions. What one society deems virtuous, another might consider morally ambiguous or even reprehensible.

This inherent variability underscores the contextual nature of ethical frameworks and highlights the absence of a universally agreed-upon definition. The very act of defining "good" inherently necessitates a corresponding definition of "evil," and that creates a dynamic, often opposing, duality.

Consider the concept of dietary restrictions. In many Abrahamic traditions, the consumption of pork is forbidden, a precept rooted in specific religious texts and interpretations. However, in numerous other cultures, pork is a staple food, integrated into culinary traditions and viewed as a source of nourishment without moral consequence. This seemingly simple example reveals a profound difference in ethical frameworks, based on cultural and religious perspectives. The act of consuming pork, therefore, carries vastly different moral values depending on the individual's cultural or religious background.

Similarly, the concept of violence reveals stark contrasts in moral interpretation. While most societies condemn unprovoked aggression and murder, the justification of violence in self-defense, warfare, or even capital punishment remains a hotly debated topic.

The ethical implications of warfare, for example, have been pondered by philosophers and theologians for millennia. The just war theory, a prominent philosophical framework, attempts to delineate conditions under which warfare might be morally justifiable. However, even within this framework, there remains considerable debate regarding the proportionality of force, the targeting of civilians, and generally the ethical implications of engaging in armed conflict. The very definition of "just" becomes a fluid concept, dependent on individual perspectives, cultural norms, and the specific context of the conflict.

Furthermore, the ethical implications of economic systems often reveal significant moral ambiguities. Capitalism, for instance, generating immense wealth and innovation, has also been criticized for perpetuating inequality, exploitation, and environmental degradation. Conversely, socialist and communist ideologies, while aiming for greater equality and social justice, have historically faced challenges regarding individual liberties and economic efficiency. The evaluation of these systems often relies on subjective interpretations of justice, fairness, and society's overall well-being. There is no singular, universally accepted metric by which to judge the moral superiority of one system over another.

The impact of technological advancements further complicates the understanding of good and evil. Medical technology, for instance, offers the potential to extend life and alleviate suffering, yet it also raises ethical questions regarding end-of-life care, genetic engineering, and allocation of scarce resources. Similarly, advancements in artificial intelligence and robotics introduce complex moral dilemmas regarding autonomy, responsibility, and the potential for unforeseen consequences. The rapid pace of technological change often outstrips our ability to develop comprehensive ethical frameworks to guide its responsible application, and this leads to continuous and evolving moral debates.

Even within a single religious tradition, the interpretation of good and evil can vary significantly. Different denominations and sects within Christianity, Islam, and Buddhism, for example, may hold contrasting views on issues such as abortion, euthanasia, and the role of women in religious leadership. These internal variations highlight the interpretive nature of religious texts, and the influence of cultural and historical contexts on theological understanding.

The inherent ambiguity and interpretative flexibility within religious texts often lead to a plurality of viewpoints, further complicating the universal definition of good and evil.

Furthermore, the temporal dimension adds another layer of complexity. Actions deemed morally acceptable in one historical era may be considered reprehensible in another. The historical acceptance of slavery, for instance, stands in stark contrast to modern abolitionist movements. This evolution of moral understanding underscores the dynamic and contextual nature of ethical frameworks, and highlights the influence of societal norms, scientific understanding, and evolving perspectives on human rights.

The personal experiences and values of individuals also profoundly shape their perception of good and evil. A person raised in a culture that emphasizes collectivism may define good actions differently from someone raised in an individualistic culture. Personal experiences with suffering, injustice, and loss can also profoundly influence one's moral compass. This can lead to nuanced perspectives that defy easy categorization. These personal and subjective influences highlight the limitations of attempting to impose a singular, universal definition of good and evil.

The challenge, therefore, lies not in seeking a definitive, universally applicable definition of good and evil, but rather in fostering a deeper understanding of the diverse perspectives and contextual nuances that shape our moral judgments. We can engage in critical reflection and with diverse viewpoints and even cultivate empathy as crucial steps in navigating the complex moral landscape; all in a bid to foster a more just and compassionate world. The journey towards ethical understanding is not a destination, but an ongoing process of learning, questioning, and refining our moral compass in the face of constant change and evolving understanding. This continuous dialogue, the constant striving for a more nuanced understanding, is itself the path towards a more ethically informed life. The pursuit of good, therefore, becomes a journey of continuous self-reflection, and engagement with the multifaceted reality of human experience.

The Moral Compass: Navigating Ethical Dilemmas

The inherent ambiguity of moral choices becomes starkly apparent when we move beyond simple pronouncements of good and evil and delve into the complexities of real-world ethical dilemmas. These are not abstract philosophical exercises but difficult decisions we face daily in our personal and professional lives, and as citizens of a global community. The absence of a universal moral code makes it necessary to develop frameworks to guide us in navigating these challenges. Utilitarianism, deontology, and virtue ethics offer contrasting, yet valuable, perspectives.

Utilitarianism, with its emphasis on maximizing general happiness and minimizing suffering, presents a seemingly straightforward approach. However, the practical application of utilitarianism is fraught with difficulties. Consider the classic "trolley problem," where a runaway trolley is heading towards five people, but you can divert it to a track where only one person will be killed. A utilitarian calculation might favor sacrificing one life to save five, prioritizing the greater good. Yet, this conclusion sits uneasily with many, raising questions about the inherent value of individual lives and the potential for unintended consequences. Furthermore, it is often impossible to predict the outcomes of actions with complete accuracy, which makes a purely utilitarian assessment highly problematic.

The complexities of assigning numerical values to happiness and suffering also undermine the practicality of this approach in many real-world situations. For example, how do we quantify the suffering of a family whose member is lost in a preventable accident, versus the economic gains of a factory that would endanger them? The inherent subjectivity involved significantly limits the efficacy of a purely utilitarian approach.

Deontology, on the other hand, emphasizes adherence to moral duties and rules, regardless of the consequences. Immanuel Kant's categorical imperative, a cornerstone of deontological ethics, posits that we should act only according to principles that could rationally become universal laws. This framework offers a compelling moral compass, and emphasizes the importance of principles such as honesty, justice, and respect for people. However, deontology can also lead to rigid adherence to rules, which may not always be appropriate in specific circumstances. The conflict between duty and consequence can be particularly challenging. For example, imagine a doctor knowing that providing certain life-extending treatments would, in the long term, cause significantly more suffering for the patient. Following the deontological principle of preserving life above all else might result in perpetuating a prolonged period of severe distress. Such situations expose limitations within deontological frameworks. The inflexible nature of strict rules often clashes with the exigencies of real-life scenarios.

Virtue ethics, unlike the other two, focuses on the character of the moral agent rather than the action itself. It emphasizes the cultivation of virtues such as honesty, courage, compassion, and justice. This perspective places strong emphasis on personal growth, self-reflection, and the development of moral character. The cultivation of virtuous character, however, is a lifelong process that requires continuous self-assessment and adaptation. The challenge lies in determining which virtues are the most important in specific contexts, and how to balance competing virtues. For example, should one prioritize honesty even if it is likely to cause significant harm? Should one always be compassionate even at the expense of justice? These internal conflicts highlight the fact that the decision to choose a virtuous action is not always clear-cut. While virtue ethics avoids the pitfalls associated with adherence to strict rules, it fails to establish a concrete metric that would help one define and choose a path toward virtuous action.

When we apply these frameworks to real-world dilemmas, their inherent limitations and the persistent complexities of ethical decision-making come to the fore. Consider the ethical challenges surrounding medical resource allocation. Medical personnel face difficult moral choices in situations of scarcity, when they must prioritize patients based on factors such as age, likelihood of recovery, or social contribution. A utilitarian approach might advocate for maximization of the number of lives saved, even if it means denying treatment to some individuals. Meanwhile, a deontological perspective might emphasize the equal moral worth of all individuals, and, therefore, advocate for a fair and equitable distribution of the resources available, regardless of the magnitude or importance of individual outcomes. In the virtue ethic approach, one might focus on the character and values of the healthcare providers, hence emphasize compassion, fairness, and responsible decision-making within that framework of limited resources. Whatever approach is at play, the decision entails difficult choices and inevitable compromises.

Furthermore, when trying to navigate ethical dilemmas, the role of cultural and religious perspectives cannot be ignored. Different cultures may interpret acceptable behavior differently, just as religious traditions often vary in the guidance they offer on moral issues, sometimes within the same tradition.

The situation becomes even more complex due to the tension between universal ethical principles and culturally specific norms. For example, while many societies condemn the practice of female genital mutilation, the continued practice in some cultures underscores the clash between universal human rights and deeply ingrained cultural traditions. While it is imperative that we respect cultural diversity, it is a challenge to determine how to protect human rights without promoting cultural imperialism. The intersection of personal faith and moral action creates numerous difficulties, especially when religious convictions clash with universal moral principles. The same difficulties arise when different religious interpretations dictate contradictory actions.

Moreover, the rapid pace of technological advancement introduces new ethical dilemmas that were previously unimaginable. Advances in artificial intelligence, genetic engineering, and reproductive technologies challenge existing ethical frameworks, and necessitate the development of new ones. The potential benefits of these technologies are immense, yet their misuse can have catastrophic consequences. Autonomous weapons systems, for instance, raise questions about accountability and the potential for unintended harm. There are also concerns about the very nature of warfare. The ethical implications of genetic manipulation pose complex challenges related to human dignity, individual autonomy, and long-term consequences for society. The challenge is to harness the benefits of these technologies while mitigating the risks. The process requires careful consideration of ethical implications, and development of robust regulatory frameworks.

To navigate these intricate moral landscapes, one requires a deep understanding of ethical frameworks and a willingness to engage in critical reflection, empathy, and dialogue. There are no easy answers or simple solutions. The process of ethical decision-making requires humility, recognition that our own perspectives are limited, and commitment to continuous learning and dialogue with others. The development of sound moral judgment is a continuous process of self-reflection, and it also requires engagement with the multifaceted realities of human experience. This is informed by ethical frameworks, guided by empathy, and shaped by societal and cultural contexts.

The pursuit of a more just and ethical world is, therefore, a journey of continuous refinement, adjustment, and a deep commitment to the ongoing pursuit of moral understanding. In a world where complexities are ever evolving, the ability to critically assess, evaluate, and respond to ethical challenges remains a crucial skill; perhaps the most crucial skill of all.

The Consequences of Our Actions Shaping Our Destiny

As we have seen, the exploration of good and evil is not a simple matter that can be viewed in black and white. Ethical frameworks offer valuable tools for navigating moral dilemmas, but their inherent limitations underscore the profound complexity of human action and its consequences. This complexity extends beyond the immediate repercussions of our choices and reaches into the very fabric of our being. According to many belief systems, it shapes our destiny, both in this life and beyond. The concept of karma, or divine justice, offers one such lens through which to examine these long-term consequences.

While the specifics vary across different traditions, the core principle of karma rests on the premise that our actions create ripples whose impact can be felt long after. It is not a matter of direct cause and effect as understood in the physical sense, but a deeper, more holistic connection between our choices and the unfolding of our lives. While this process can be understood as a linear sequence, it is also a complex web of interconnectedness, where seemingly insignificant actions can have unforeseen and far-reaching consequences. A single act of kindness, for instance, can trigger a chain of positive reactions, as witnessed in subsequent positive events. These happenings not only impact the immediate recipient, but also the people around them; with the potential to extend across generations. Conversely, a seemingly small act of cruelty can have devastating ramifications. Such negative consequences can echo through the lives of those affected, with the potential to create cycles of suffering.

The emphasis on personal accountability is central to the concept of karma. We are not merely passive recipients of fate; we actively shape our destiny through our choices. This reality underscores the profound responsibility we carry each moment and encourages careful consideration of the impact our actions have on others and ourselves. The idea is not simply about one reaping what they sow in a simplistic, transactional way. Instead, it is about highlighting the transformative power our actions have on our own inner landscape. Repeated acts of generosity, compassion, and mindfulness cultivate inner peace and harmony, while consistent selfishness and cruelty often lead to internal conflict and suffering.

Consider the example of someone who consistently lies. Such an individual often manages to avoid uncomfortable situations – that is the immediate consequence. However, that short-term advantage does not guarantee them future freedom or peace. Over time, people may begin to lose trust in them, something that may damage existing relationships. People prone to lying may also experience internal dissonance that comes with living a life of deception, which can lead to profound isolation and unhappiness. The "karma," in this case, is not a supernatural retribution, but the natural consequence of the liar's actions – the self-inflicted wound of a life lived inauthentically. Similarly, the individual who prioritizes self-improvement, learning, and personal growth, might experience challenges and setbacks along the way, but the long-term benefits – increased competence, stronger relationships, and a greater sense of fulfillment – are often seen as a positive form of "karmic reward." These are not rewards given by a higher power, but the natural outcomes of aligning one's actions with personal and spiritual growth.

In many spiritual traditions, the concept of karma extends beyond a single lifetime. The idea of reincarnation, for instance, suggests that the consequences of our actions reverberate across multiple lifetimes. Past actions shape our current circumstances, while our current actions will determine our future experiences. This perspective emphasizes the importance of seeking not only immediate gratification, but also long-term spiritual growth and transformation. The goal is not merely to avoid negative consequences, but to cultivate virtuous qualities that lead to greater inner peace and harmony. This ongoing process of refinement and purification is a central aspect of the karmic journey.

The interpretation of karma, however, often varies across different belief systems. Some traditions focus heavily on retribution, and emphasize the idea that negative actions inevitably lead to suffering. Others place more emphasis on the transformative power of our actions, viewing karma as a learning process that allows us to evolve spiritually. Still, others might view karma as a complex interplay of individual agency and divine grace, suggesting that while our actions have consequences, divine intervention can also influence the outcome. The differences in these interpretations underscore the multifaceted nature of the concept and highlight the importance of understanding the specific nuances of different belief systems when discussing karma.

Regardless of specific theological perspectives, the principle of accountability remains paramount. The concept of karma encourages introspection, urging us to reflect on our choices and their impact. It invites us to consider the ethical implications of our actions, not just in terms of their immediate consequences, but also in relation to their long-term effects on ourselves and others. This emphasis on self-reflection is a crucial element of personal growth and spiritual development. Regular introspection helps to cultivate greater awareness of our own motivations and patterns of behavior, and allows us to identify areas where we need to make changes.

Furthermore, understanding karma promotes empathy and compassion. When we recognize the interconnectedness of all beings and the far-reaching consequences of our actions, we become more mindful of the impact of our choices on others. This fosters a greater sense of responsibility towards our community and the world at large. This concept motivates actions informed by consideration and a deep sense of interconnectedness, rather than self-serving desires. In a world often characterized by short-term thinking and immediate gratification, this longer-term view of consequences becomes vital.

In many spiritual traditions, practices such as meditation, mindfulness, and prayer are used to cultivate a deeper awareness of our actions and their consequences. These practices aid in cultivating self-awareness and fostering a more ethical and compassionate approach to life. These practices are not merely religious rituals; they are tools for self-reflection and personal growth that allow individuals to align their actions with their values and intentions. They provide an avenue for examining one's own behavior patterns, helping individuals to understand the underlying causes of their actions.

The concept of karma, therefore, transcends merely religious dogma. It offers a powerful framework within which to understand the profound relationship between our actions and our destiny. It also emphasizes the importance of personal accountability, self-reflection, and compassion, and serves as a reminder that our choices are not isolated events but integral parts of a larger tapestry of interconnectedness. This means they shape not only our own lives, but also the lives of others and the world around us. The ongoing engagement with this concept offers a continuous path toward personal growth, a journey of refinement and a deeper understanding of our place in the cosmos. It is not a journey of fearful retribution, but of mindful action and compassionate living. It is one guided by the understanding that our choices, no matter how seemingly small, echo through time and space, and shape the destiny we ultimately create. The exploration of karma, therefore, is not merely an academic exercise, but a vital guide to help us navigate the complex landscape of morality, while shaping a life of meaning and purpose.

Redemption and Forgiveness: The Path to Spiritual Renewal

The exploration of karma and its implications lead naturally to a discussion about redemption and forgiveness, two concepts intimately linked to the idea of spiritual renewal. While the concept of karma emphasizes the consequences of our actions, the possibilities of redemption and forgiveness offer pathways toward healing individually and collectively. These are not merely theological abstractions, but deeply human experiences that reflect our inherent desire for reconciliation, and the possibility of a second chance.

The understanding of redemption varies significantly across different religious and philosophical traditions. In some Abrahamic faiths, for instance, redemption is often understood through the lens of divine grace and atonement. The concept of sacrifice, particularly the sacrificial death of Jesus Christ in Christianity, plays a pivotal role in the narrative of redemption. This act is seen as a means of expiating humanity's sins and offering a pathway to reconciliation with God. Repentance, a sincere turning away from wrongdoing, accompanied by a commitment to a more righteous life, becomes a crucial component of this process. This is not simply a matter of seeking forgiveness but actively engaging in transformative change.

The emphasis is on genuine internal transformation, not merely superficial adjustments in behavior.

Other religions, such as Buddhism, offer a different perspective on redemption. The Buddhist path to liberation, or Nirvana, involves a systematic process of self-cultivation through practices such as meditation, mindfulness, and ethical conduct. Redemption, in this context, is not necessarily tied to the forgiveness of sins, but to the gradual eradication of suffering through the overcoming of negative karmic tendencies. The emphasis is on personal responsibility and the cultivation of positive qualities like compassion, wisdom, and generosity. Through diligent practice, individuals gradually purify their minds and transcend the cycle of suffering, ultimately achieving liberation. This process is a continuous journey of self-improvement, not a single event of atonement.

The philosophical perspectives on redemption also exhibit considerable diversity. Some secular ethical frameworks emphasize the importance of making amends for past mistakes and still emphasize the restorative justice approach where one repairs any harm caused, even as they take responsibility for their actions. This may involve making reparations to those harmed, publicly acknowledging the wrongdoing, and committing to change behavior; commitment being a way to prevent future harm. The focus is less on divine intervention or spiritual purification and more on practical steps towards ethical reconciliation.

Forgiveness, intricately interwoven with redemption, is another multifaceted concept with significant theological and philosophical implications. The capacity to forgive, both oneself and others, is often considered a crucial element of spiritual growth and emotional well-being.

Forgiving oneself recognizes that past mistakes do not define one's entire identity. It also allows for self-compassion and a release from the burden of guilt and shame. This process, however, often requires a deep examination of one's actions and their consequences, accepting responsibility for the harm caused, and making a commitment to positive change.

Forgiving others, challenging as it may appear, can be equally transformative. It can be emotionally draining and ultimately self-destructive to hold onto resentment and anger. Forgiveness does not necessarily mean condoning the actions of the offending party but rather releasing the grip of negative emotions that comes with holding onto grudges. It also means moving towards a more peaceful state of mind. Forgiving does not diminish the gravity of the offense committed, but it frees the victim from the shackles of anger and hatred while promoting healing and reconciliation. It is important to note that forgiveness is a process as opposed to a single event, and, therefore, it can take time. Sometimes it also takes effort to let go of resentment.

The relationship between redemption and forgiveness highlights the ongoing process of spiritual growth and moral development.

Redemption is not a one-time achievement, but an ongoing journey of self-improvement and ethical living. It is about being proactive in trying to improve oneself, acknowledge past mistakes, and avoiding repeating them. This involves continuous self-reflection, commitment to personal growth, and willingness to accept the consequences of one's actions; all the while striving to attain positive change.

Within many religious frameworks, the concept of divine grace or divine intervention plays a significant role in the understanding of redemption. The concept suggests that God's unconditional love and mercy can help overcome even the most significant of transgressions. This does not negate the importance of repentance or personal responsibility. Rather, it emphasizes the transformative power of divine intervention in restoring a broken relationship. This grace, however, is not taken as passive acceptance of wrongdoing. Instead, it is considered an enabling force that empowers individuals to engage in the process of self-improvement and ethical living.

The question of whether forgiveness is possible for the unforgivable or deplorable acts is a complex one, and it continues to be a subject of debate within theological and philosophical circles. The concept of restorative justice offers a pragmatic approach and focuses on repairing the harm caused rather than focusing on the abstract notion of forgiveness. This requires that individuals take practical steps to address the impact of their wrongdoing and make amends to those affected. This creates a path toward reconciliation even in the most severe of cases. It acknowledges the limitations of forgiveness as a concept and offers an alternative framework to help achieve resolution and healing.

The spiritual practices of different traditions often provide tools to facilitate the process of redemption and forgiveness. Meditation, for instance, can help cultivate self-awareness and compassion, two components that are essential in forgiving, not only oneself, but others. Prayers can facilitate connection with higher power and provide a space for seeking guidance and strength during times of struggle. Acts of service and compassion towards others can also be powerfully transformative, and they offer a tangible way to express remorse and make amends.

It is crucial to understand that the processes of redemption and forgiveness are not always easy. They often involve confronting difficult emotions, acknowledging past mistakes, and committing to significant changes in behavior and attitude. This journey may involve seeking professional help, engaging in therapy or counseling, and building supportive relationships with trusted individuals. The path to spiritual renewal is not a solitary one. It often requires support from the community and the guidance of mentors or spiritual advisors.

The concept of redemption and forgiveness ultimately touches upon the very core of human experience and reflects our capacity for both wrongdoing and self-improvement. It underscores the inherent human desire for reconciliation, healing, and second chance. Whether approached through a religious, philosophical, or secular lens, the journey towards redemption and forgiveness is a path towards personal growth. It fosters greater self-understanding, compassion, and a deeper connection with oneself and others. It is a journey that underscores the dynamic nature of the human spirit, its ability to learn and grow, and ultimately transform itself even in the face of profound mistakes.

The exploration of this journey should not be perceived as a search for simplistic answers, but a continuous process of self-discovery and moral development. It is a path toward spiritual renewal that offers hope and transformation for both the individual and society. It is a journey worth undertaking because it is at the heart of what makes us human – that capacity we have for both fallibility and profound transformation.

The Nature of Temptation: Resisting External Influences

The previous discussion of karma, redemption, and forgiveness laid the groundwork to help us understand the internal struggle inherent in navigating the landscape of good and evil. However, the moral landscape is not solely an internal terrain. It is also shaped by external forces that constantly test our resolve and challenge our ethical commitments. This subsection delves into the nature of temptation and explores the external influences that can sway our moral choices. It also examines the strategies individuals can employ to resist these pressures and maintain their ethical compass.

Temptation, in its broadest sense, represents an external appeal to act against one's better judgment, or established moral code. It manifests in countless forms, ranging from subtle suggestions to overt pressures; and they all vie for our attention while trying to influence our decisions. These influences can originate from a variety of sources: societal expectations, peer pressure, the allure of material possessions, the pursuit of power, or the simple desire for immediate gratification. Understanding the nature of these external forces is crucial to developing effective strategies for resistance.

Societal pressures often exert powerful influence on individual moral choices. For example, the norms and values prevalent in a particular culture or community can shape our perceptions of right and wrong and influence our behavior and choices even when these norms conflict with our personal ethical compass. Conformity, the desire to fit into our social groups, can lead individuals to compromise their values, and engage in actions they might otherwise deem unethical. This pressure is particularly acute during periods of social upheaval or uncertainty, when established norms are challenged or weakened. The history of totalitarian regimes provides chilling examples of how societal pressure can erode individual morality and compel individuals to participate in acts of cruelty and injustice against their own better judgment.

Peer pressure, a specific form of societal influence, often targets young people whose moral compass is still developing. The desire for acceptance among one's peers can lead adolescents and young adults to engage in risky behaviors, such as substance abuse, reckless driving, or vandalism, even if they recognize the inherent dangers and moral implications. The fear of ostracism, rejection, or ridicule can be a powerful motivator. It can drive individuals to conform to group norms even when those norms conflict with their personal values. This is especially pronounced in situations where social status and acceptance are highly valued within the group.

Material possessions and the relentless pursuit of wealth can also act as powerful temptations. Consumer culture, driven by advertising and marketing, constantly bombards individuals with messages that promote the acquisition of goods and services as the path to happiness and fulfillment. This can lead to materialistic values, where one prioritizes financial success and material possessions over ethical considerations and genuine human connections. The insatiable desire for more things can cloud judgment and lead individuals to compromise their values. Hence, they can find themselves engaging in unethical behavior such as cheating, fraud, or exploitation of others for personal gain. This constant barrage of consumerism can erode our sense of contentment and lead to a never-ending cycle, where we keep wanting more, regardless of the ethical costs.

The lustful pursuit of power, another potent external influence, can significantly corrupt moral judgment. It can cloud ethical reasoning and make individuals engage in manipulative tactics, suppress dissent, and disregard the well-being of others; all in a bid to achieve their ambitions. History is replete with examples of individuals and institutions that have sacrificed ethical principles in their relentless quest for power. Often, their actions have led to devastating consequences for themselves and others. This pursuit often involves distortion of reality, where in every instance the end justifies the meaning regardless of ethical repercussions.

The desire for immediate gratification is a fundamental human drive that can also lead individuals astray. It is an inherent tendency that prioritizes short-term pleasures over long-term consequences, and it can lead to impulsive actions and regrettable decisions. The inability to delay gratification often results in impulsive behaviors that have significant ethical implications, such as infidelity, reckless spending, and substance abuse. Understanding this aspect of human nature is critical if you want to develop strategies to counteract the influence of instant gratification.

Resisting external influences require a multifaceted approach that draws on both psychological and spiritual resources. The first critical step is to develop strong self-awareness. By cultivating a deep understanding of one's own values, beliefs, and motivations, individuals can identify potential areas of vulnerability and anticipate situations where temptation might arise. This self-knowledge becomes a powerful tool that empowers the individual, so they can make conscious choices that align with their ethical commitments rather than reacting impulsively to external pressures.

In order to navigate the complexities of the moral landscape, it is essential to cultivate strong moral principles that are not merely abstract concepts; rather, deeply ingrained values that guide decision-making. The capacity to discern what is right and wrong is rooted in a well-defined ethical framework, which provides a solid foundation for resisting temptations and adhering to one's moral compass, even under immense pressure.

Another crucial element in resisting temptation is strengthening self-discipline. Self-discipline is the ability to control one's impulses and to adhere to a chosen course of action, and it is cultivated through consistent practice and self-reflection. One must set personal boundaries, avoid tempting situations, and develop mechanisms to handle and cope with challenging situations. Engaging in regular practices, such as meditation and mindfulness, can enhance self-awareness and strengthen self-control.

One can also seek support from trusted mentors, friends, or spiritual advisors, an invaluable action in navigating the challenges of temptation. These individuals can offer guidance, encouragement, and accountability, and be a great support system to the individual; helping them stay true to their ethical commitments. The power of community in promoting ethical conduct is significant, and when individuals surround themselves with positive influences, it can bolster their own resolve.

It is also imperative that one develops empathy and compassion for others, if they are to resist temptations to exploit or harm them. Also, individuals can strengthen their resolve to act ethically if they acknowledge the human cost of unethical actions. One's capacity for empathy allows them to see the consequences of their actions on others and makes unethical behavior less appealing.

Finally, if individuals can foster a sense of spiritual connection, regardless of religious affiliation, it can become the powerful source of strength and guidance that helps them resist temptation. Fostering such a connection might involve prayer, meditation, or engagement in acts of service and compassion. If one can cultivate a deeper understanding of their purpose and place in the world, this awareness is likely to lead to a more profound commitment to ethical behavior. The spiritual connection becomes the source of inner strength that helps to navigate moral challenges and overcome temptation.

The nature of temptation is complex and multifaceted, and it constantly tests the boundaries of individual morality. For one to resist external influences and uphold their ethical commitment, it requires a combination of self-awareness, strong moral principles, self-discipline, supportive relationships, empathy, and a deeper sense of spiritual connection. It is a continuous journey that requires vigilance, self-reflection, and a commitment to living a life aligned with one's deepest values. This path is not always easy, but it ultimately leads to personal growth, spiritual fulfillment, and a more just and ethical world.

Stages of Spiritual Development: Personal Growth

In this chapter, we are going to build upon the previous discussion on temptation, and the strategies that can help resist its allure. In this regard, we are going to consider the multifaceted journey of spiritual growth.

This journey is not anything close to linear progression. On the contrary, it is a complex, and often unpredictable, path, marked by profound challenges and exhilarating breakthroughs. It is a process of continuous transformation, a gradual unfolding of the soul's inherent potential that is shaped by the cumulative experiences of a lifetime.

One can conceptualize spiritual development as a series of stages, each representing a significant shift in consciousness and understanding. These stages are not rigidly defined, nor are they necessarily experienced sequentially by all individuals. The pace of spiritual growth varies greatly depending on individual temperament, life circumstances, and the level of commitment to the process. However, certain common themes and characteristics emerge and offer a framework that helps understand this transformative journey.

The initial stage, often characterized by a naive or unquestioning acceptance of established beliefs and traditions, might be termed the Stage of Unknowing. In this phase, individuals often operate within a pre-defined framework of religious or philosophical dogma, where they accept the givens without critical inquiry. This is not necessarily a negative state. Rather, it provides a foundation upon which later stages of development can build. The reliance on external authorities and established doctrines can provide comfort and a sense of belonging, although it does not let one engage deeply at a personal level with the underlying principles. This stage is often marked by a relatively uncritical acceptance of societal norms and religious teachings. For example, individuals raised within strictly orthodox religious traditions often do not question the tenets of their faith. The focus remains largely on outward adherence to rituals and traditions, and not an inner understanding of them. There is little exploration of personal beliefs or values outside the accepted framework.

As individuals mature and encounter life's complexities, they begin to question the accepted narratives, and this marks the transition to the Stage of Questioning; a period of doubt and uncertainty. The comfortable certainty of the previous stage gives way to a critical examination of established beliefs and traditions. This questioning might be triggered by personal experiences, encounters with differing perspectives, or a growing sense of cognitive dissonance.

The individual begins to grapple with contradictions and inconsistencies within the existing framework, and this leads to a period of internal conflict and soul-searching. This stage is crucial, but often painful as it is characterized by a sense of disorientation and uncertainty. The individual may experience a crisis of faith or be disillusioned with previously held beliefs. They might actively seek out alternative perspectives and explore different philosophies and religious traditions. An example is where someone grapples with the contradictions apparent between scientific findings and religious doctrines. Other times, one may question the morality of certain practices within their own faith community.

Another phase, the Stage of Seeking, emerges naturally from the stage of questioning.

Driven by a deep desire for meaning and understanding, the individual actively seeks answers, and tries to explore diverse spiritual paths and philosophical perspectives. This is a period of intense learning and exploration, characterized by a willingness to engage with unfamiliar ideas and experiences. The individual might delve into the study of comparative religions, engage in meditative practices, or seek guidance from spiritual mentors or teachers. This process often involves experimentation, where one tries out different approaches and practices to establish what resonates with their personal truth. The emphasis shifts from passive acceptance to active engagement with the spiritual quest. This might involve intensive study of sacred texts, participation in spiritual retreats, or a search for guidance from spiritual teachers. This period is aptly exemplified when individuals embark on pilgrimages, explore various meditation techniques, or study different mystical traditions.

Once a deeper understanding begins to emerge, the individual enters the Stage of Integration. This is a stage of synthesis, where the insights gained from the previous stages are integrated into a coherent and personalized spiritual framework. The individual begins to articulate their own unique understanding of life's purpose and meaning, drawing upon their experiences and learnings. During this stage, one consolidates the knowledge and experiences acquired in the seeking phase and creates a unified and meaningful personal philosophy. This individual then moves beyond simple acceptance or questioning and proceeds to develop their own unique spiritual path that involves integration of various beliefs and practices. Ultimately, they could end up with a renewed commitment to a previously held faith, develop a personalized spiritual practice, or create a unique philosophical perspective. This stage can be seen clearly through individuals who develop their own unique form of meditation, integrate elements from different spiritual traditions into personal practice, or articulate their own spiritual philosophy.

From the stage of integration comes the Stage of Service, which represents the culmination of the previous stages. Here, the individual's deepened spiritual understanding manifests itself through action and service to others, with emphasis shifting from personal growth to outward contribution. The individual seeks to share their wisdom and compassion with the world and works towards the betterment of humanity and the planet. This stage involves acting on the spiritual understanding developed in previous stages, marked by the individual's dedication to the welfare of others. Such dedication can take many forms, such as volunteer work, charitable activities, advocacy for social justice, or environmental protection.

Beyond this, some scholars posit a further stage of Transcendence. which can be considered the final stage. Here, the individual moves beyond the limitations of the ego, and experiences a deep sense of unity with all beings and the Divine. This is a state of profound spiritual awakening, often described as merging with the ultimate reality. It is a highly advanced stage characterized by a profound sense of connection with the Divine, where ego's boundaries are dissolved. This stage is often described in mystical traditions, where one's experiences are difficult to articulate. Often the experiences are simply said to be ineffable or beyond the limits of ordinary language. This stage can be exemplified by scenarios portrayed in mystical traditions, which involve a sense of cosmic unity, profound peace, and obliteration of the boundaries of the self.

It is crucial to remember that these stages are not rigid or sequential.

Individuals may revisit earlier stages and experience them simultaneously, or progress through them at different rates. The journey is profoundly personal, and shaped by individual experiences, challenges, and spiritual aspirations. The essence of the journey does not lie solely in reaching a specific stage, but rather in the continued process of growth, transformation, and deepening connection with oneself and the Divine.

It is a continuous unfolding, a dynamic interplay between the internal and external worlds that shapes and refines the soul throughout one's life journey. The goal is not necessarily to reach a final, static state, but to engage in the transformative process itself. This means constantly striving for greater understanding, compassion, and unity, the journey itself being the destination.

The Impact of Relationships: Shaping Our Spiritual Path

Having understood the stages of spiritual growth, we now delve into the crucial role relationships play in shaping our spiritual journey. Our connections with others, whether familial, romantic, or platonic, are not merely social interactions. They are powerful catalysts for growth that offer profound challenges as well as invaluable opportunities for self-discovery and transformation. The crucible of human relationships refines the soul, reveals our strengths and weaknesses, and pushes us beyond our comfort zones. Ultimately, it fosters compassion, empathy, and a deeper understanding of ourselves and the Divine.

Family relationships, often the first and most enduring connections we forge, provide the foundational framework for our understanding of love, belonging, and connection. These early relationships, whether marked by harmony or conflict, profoundly impact on our capacity for intimacy, trust, and self-worth. A supportive family environment, characterized by unconditional love and acceptance, can provide a secure base from which to explore the world and develop a strong sense of self.

Conversely, dysfunctional family dynamics, characterized by conflict, abuse, or neglect, can create deep-seated wounds, which hinder spiritual growth and lead to feelings of insecurity, resentment, and a diminished sense of self-worth. The healing of these wounds often becomes a significant aspect of the spiritual journey, and it requires self-awareness, forgiveness, and a willingness to confront the past.

This reality is reflected in individuals with childhood trauma work through their experiences in therapy as they explore their emotions through journaling or creative expression or seek solace and healing through spiritual practices like prayer or meditation. The process is often long and arduous and requires courage and patience. and deep commitment to personal healing.

Romantic relationships present another potent arena for spiritual growth. The intensity of intimacy and vulnerability inherent in these connections reveals our capacity for love, and our shadow selves. As we navigate the complexities of romantic partnerships, we are challenged to confront our fears, insecurities, and attachment patterns. Healthy romantic relationships can foster mutual growth, and offer support, encouragement, and a safe space for self-expression. They can also inspire us to become more compassionate, understanding, and selfless.

However, unhealthy relationships, marked by control, manipulation, or abuse, can impede spiritual growth, and create cycles of negativity and self-doubt. The ability to discern health from unhealthy relationships, set healthy boundaries, and move on from destructive partnerships, is a critical component of spiritual maturity. This often involves recognizing and addressing patterns of codependency, developing healthy communication skills, and learning to prioritize one's own well-being.

Leaving a toxic relationship can be a significant spiritual act, a courageous assertion of self-worth, and a step toward creating a life aligned with one's deepest values. Learning to forgive oneself and one's partner is equally crucial. This is not about condoning harmful behavior but releasing the emotional burdens of the past in order to move towards healthier relationships in the future.

Platonic friendships, while often overlooked, also contribute significantly to our spiritual journey. They offer companionship, support, and opportunities for growth, through shared experiences and mutual learning. Meaningful friendships provide a space for authentic self-expression and challenge us to be vulnerable and open to feedback. They can also serve as a mirror, where they reflect our strengths and weaknesses and prompt us to examine our behaviors and attitudes. Supportive friends can offer encouragement during challenging times, and keep reminding us of our inherent worth, while inspiring us to persevere. However, unhealthy friendships, marked by negativity, judgment, or manipulation, can deplete our energy, and hinder our growth.

For the sake of our spiritual well-being, it is crucial that we learn to choose our friends wisely, nurture healthy relationships, and let go of those that no longer serve our well-being. We need to recognize the importance of mutual respect, open communication, and shared values, in forming lasting and meaningful connections. It is of paramount importance that we learn to cultivate healthy boundaries in friendships, avoid people-pleasing tendencies, and prioritize genuine connections over superficial ones.

Beyond these types of primary relationships, the impact extends to broader communities and encounters with strangers. The way we interact with colleagues, neighbors, and the wider world reveals our level of compassion, empathy, and understanding. Acts of kindness, generosity, and service to others become expressions of our spiritual growth and reflect a deepened connection to something larger than ourselves. Even seemingly insignificant interactions can be opportunities for spiritual development, providing opportunities to practice patience, forgiveness, and compassion.

Engaging with those that hold different perspectives can challenge our beliefs and expand our understanding of the world and humanity's diverse experiences. It is a hallmark of spiritual maturity to be able to navigate disagreements with grace and respect, engage in meaningful dialogue, and cultivate a spirit of tolerance and understanding. The ability to find common ground with those who hold different viewpoints is a testament to our spiritual growth and reflects an expansion of our empathy and compassion. This includes acknowledging the value of diverse perspectives, practicing active listening, and engaging in constructive dialogue even when disagreements arise.

The relationships we cultivate throughout our lives are not merely social constructs; they are integral to our spiritual evolution. They challenge us, teach us, and push us to grow in ways we otherwise might not. The journey of self-discovery is profoundly intertwined with the relationships we form and nurture and learning to navigate the complexities of these connections with wisdom, compassion, and self-awareness becomes a crucial aspect of our spiritual quest. Ultimately, it leads to a deeper understanding of ourselves, our place in the world, and the divine reality that permeates all of existence. By cultivating healthy, nurturing relationships, while also learning to detach from those that are harmful, we pave the path for spiritual growth, and shape our souls into instruments of love, compassion, and service.

The ability to forgive, both ourselves and others, is crucial in this process, as it frees us from the burdens of the past and allows us to embrace the possibilities of the future. The transformative power of relationship, when viewed through a spiritual lens, reveals its profound and multifaceted role in our journey towards wholeness. The quality of our connections profoundly shapes the path of our spiritual growth, guiding us toward greater self-awareness, compassion, and ultimately, a deeper connection with the Divine.

Overcoming Suffering: Finding Meaning in Hardship

The tapestry of life, richly woven with threads of joy and sorrow, inevitably includes the somber hues of suffering. While we naturally recoil from hardship, spiritual traditions across millennia consistently posit suffering as a potential crucible for profound growth and transformation; not an enemy to be vanquished. This is not to romanticize pain, nor to suggest a passive acceptance of the suffering brought about by injustice. It is merely an invitation to explore the paradoxical ways in which adversity can illuminate our inner landscape and reveal hidden strengths; hence leading to a deeper appreciation of life's preciousness.

One of the most prevalent perspectives on suffering comes from the concept of karma, and is found in various Eastern traditions, particularly Hinduism, Buddhism, and Jainism. Karma is not a system of cosmic punishment, but rather a principle of cause and effect. Our actions, thoughts, and intentions create ripples in the universe, and they impact not only ourselves but others. From this perspective, suffering might be the consequence of past actions - a karmic debt being repaid.

However, this understanding does not preclude agency; instead, it empowers us to shape our future by consciously cultivating positive actions and intentions. The experience of suffering becomes an opportunity for reflection, a chance to examine our choices and make amends for any harm we have caused. This leads to a path of purification and liberation.

The Abrahamic traditions, which encompass Judaism, Christianity, and Islam, offer different, yet equally compelling, frameworks for understanding suffering. In the Hebrew Bible, the Book of Job presents a powerful exploration of the problem of suffering. It questions the relationship between divine justice and human experience. Job's unwavering faith despite immense hardship becomes a testament to the enduring power of spiritual resilience.

Christian theology often interprets suffering through the lens of Christ's crucifixion and resurrection – a model of selfless sacrifice and ultimate triumph over death and despair. The cross becomes a symbol of redemptive suffering, which suggests that even in the darkest of moments it is possible to experience hope and renewal. Similarly, Islamic teachings emphasize the importance of patience (sabr) in the face of adversity, understanding suffering as a test of faith and an opportunity to draw closer to God. These religious traditions encourage approaching suffering as a potential path to spiritual growth and connection with the Divine, and not merely as something to be endured.

Philosophically, existentialist thinkers like Søren Kierkegaard and Albert Camus grappled with the inherent absurdity of existence, and the ubiquitous presence of suffering. They emphasized the importance of individual responsibility in the face of meaninglessness, arguing that we create our own meaning and values through our choices and actions. Suffering, in this context, becomes an opportunity to confront the limitations of human existence, and to forge a path towards authenticity.

The experience of facing existential angsts, the awareness of our mortality, and the lack of inherent meaning in the universe, can paradoxically be a source of empowerment. It can, therefore, push us to define our own purpose and values. This process of self-creation, often forged in the fires of hardship, underscores the transformative potential of confronting life's inherent challenges.

Beyond theological and philosophical interpretations are psychological perspectives. These offer valuable insights into how we cope with and learn from suffering. Trauma-informed therapies, for example, acknowledge the profound impact adverse experiences have on individuals' mental and emotional well-being. These therapies provide frameworks that help understand, process, and heal from traumatic events. They foster resilience and promote emotional regulation. Mindfulness practices, such as meditation and yoga, have also been shown to increase self-awareness, emotional regulation, and stress resilience. By cultivating a present-moment awareness, individuals can better manage challenging emotions and find a sense of calm amidst chaos. These techniques empower individuals to not only survive but thrive in the face of adversity as they transform hardship into an opportunity for personal growth and emotional healing.

The path towards finding meaning in suffering is not linear; it is a journey of self-discovery, characterized by periods of intense struggle and moments of profound insight. It requires courage, resilience, and a willingness to engage with the deepest aspects of ourselves. It is crucial to acknowledge the validity of our emotions, as we allow ourselves to grieve, rage, and despair. If we suppress these feelings, we can impede the healing process, prolong suffering, and hinder our ability to move forward. On the contrary, expressing our emotions can be an essential step in processing pain and finding a path to healing. Among the various healthy outlets for our emotions are journaling, art, music, and engaging in supportive conversations with trusted friends or therapists.

The process of finding meaning in suffering is deeply personal and subjective. There is no one-size-fits-all answer; no universal formula for transforming hardship into enlightenment. What resonates with one individual may not resonate with another.

For some, the path may involve a deeper engagement with their spiritual beliefs, finding solace and strength in their faith. For others, it might involve re-evaluating their values and priorities, leading to significant life changes. Still, others may find meaning in helping others who are struggling, drawing strength and purpose from acts of compassion and service.

The capacity for empathy and compassion is often significantly amplified through suffering. Having experienced hardship, individuals frequently develop a greater understanding of human vulnerability and a heightened sensitivity to the struggles of others. This deepened empathy can motivate individuals to actively engage in acts of service, contribute to their own healing, while also making a positive impact on the world. This process of turning personal pain into positive action becomes a powerful testament to the transformative potential of suffering.

Furthermore, adversity can lead to a renewed appreciation for the simple joys of life. When faced with hardship, we often gain a clearer perspective on what truly matters. The mundane aspects of everyday life, often taken for granted, can take on new significance. This shift in perspective allows us to appreciate beauty in everyday moments, and foster gratitude and contentment. Newfound appreciation can enrich our lives in profound ways, leading to a greater sense of purpose and fulfillment.

In conclusion, the journey through suffering is rarely easy. It is a complex and nuanced process that requires self-awareness, resilience, and a willingness to engage with difficult emotions. However, by approaching hardship as a potential catalyst for growth and not as an insurmountable obstacle, we can uncover hidden strengths, deepen our understanding of ourselves and the world, and cultivate a profound appreciation for the preciousness of life. This process does not seek to avoid suffering altogether for that is almost impossible; rather, it helps one learn to navigate through difficult experiences with wisdom, compassion, and a commitment to finding meaning during adversity. The path may be challenging, but the rewards of personal transformation and a deepened connection to something larger than us can make the journey profoundly worthwhile. Suffering, when approached with intentionality and self-awareness, can become a catalyst for profound spiritual growth, and a richer, more meaningful life.

The Role of Community: Shared Spiritual Journeys

The preceding exploration of individual journeys through suffering underscores the inherent solitude that often accompanies such experiences. Yet, the human spirit, deeply relational by nature, finds solace and strength in introspection and in the embrace of community. The shared spiritual journey, undertaken alongside others grappling with similar challenges, offers a potent antidote to isolation. It also fosters resilience, empathy, and a profound sense of belonging. This communal aspect of spiritual growth is not merely a peripheral element, but an integral part of the transformative process itself.

Shared faith, within the context of religious and spiritual communities, provides a framework within which we understand and navigate suffering. The collective rituals, prayers, and shared narratives of faith offer comfort and hope, and remind individuals that they are not alone in their struggle. The belief in a higher power shared by the community serves as a guiding principle, or a transcendent reality that provides a source of meaning and purpose even amidst overwhelming hardship. This sense of connection transcends the experience of one individual and anchors the individual members within a larger narrative of faith, hope, and redemption. Consider, for instance, the support groups found within many religious congregations. These spaces, often facilitated by trained clergy or lay leaders, provide a safe environment for individuals to share their struggles in confidentiality, as they receive support and learn from the experiences of others. The shared experience of faith serves as a powerful unifier that fosters a sense of solidarity and mutual understanding.

Furthermore, shared struggles, irrespective of religious affiliation, create potent bonds of empathy and mutual support. Support groups dedicated to specific challenges – grief, addiction, chronic illness, or trauma – provide a space where individuals can openly share their vulnerabilities without judgment. The shared experience of adversity creates a powerful sense of connection and diminishes the feeling of isolation while fostering a sense of shared humanity. In these spaces, individuals discover that they are not alone in their suffering, and that their experiences are valid and understood. They also learn that healing is possible. The simple act of bearing witness to another's pain, and one's pain being witnessed in return, is profoundly healing. It is a shared vulnerability that fosters a sense of mutual respect and compassion and cultivates a supportive environment conducive to growth and healing. The recognition that others have traversed similar terrains of difficulty empowers individuals to confront their own struggles with renewed courage and hope.

The sharing of triumphs is also equally significant. As individuals navigate their spiritual journeys, moments of breakthrough, insight, and healing, inevitably emerge. The opportunity to celebrate these moments within a supportive community amplifies their significance, enriches the individual's experience, and strengthens the bonds of fellowship. Sharing stories of resilience, recovery, and transformation reinforces the message that healing is possible; that hope persists even in the darkest of times.

These narratives serve as beacons of hope and inspire others to persevere on their own journeys. They also foster a sense of collective progress.

The shared celebration of growth and healing creates a cycle of encouragement and mutual support, bolstering the overall resilience of the community. The public acknowledgement of progress not only honors individual achievement but also strengthens the communal fabric. This underscores the power of shared experience in fostering spiritual growth.

The specific forms that community takes in fostering spiritual growth are diverse and dependent on context. From formal religious organizations to informal peer support groups, from online forums to close-knit family units, the potential for spiritual nourishment within community is immense. Consider, for instance, the role of monastic orders across various religious traditions. These communities, often characterized by shared vows of poverty, chastity, and obedience, provide a structured environment for spiritual discipline and reflection. The shared life, governed by a common set of rules and values, fosters a sense of belonging and mutual support, and allows individuals to focus on their spiritual development. This happens without the distractions of worldly concerns. The structured routine, shared meditative practices, and mutual accountability contributes significantly to spiritual growth. Similarly, indigenous cultures worldwide often emphasize the importance of community rituals, ceremonies, and storytelling, all geared toward transmitting spiritual knowledge and fostering a sense of connection with the natural world and the ancestors. These practices cultivate a strong sense of identity and belonging and strengthen the individual's connection to a larger spiritual reality.

The power of community extends beyond the realm of formal religious or spiritual structures. Even secular communities can play a crucial role in supporting spiritual growth at the level of the individual. Friendship circles, support networks often built around shared interests or hobbies, and volunteer organizations, all offer opportunities for connection, mutual support, and development of empathy and compassion. The shared pursuit of common goals can foster a sense of purpose and meaning and provide a framework for personal growth and spiritual exploration.

It is a profoundly spiritual experience to contribute to something larger than oneself, and to engage in acts of service. Such contribution also nurtures compassion, selflessness, and a greater sense of interconnectedness.

In contrast, the absence of a supportive community can significantly impede spiritual growth. Isolation, loneliness, and lack of meaningful connections can exacerbate suffering, hinder the healing process, and foster feelings of despair and hopelessness. Lack of a shared framework to help understand suffering, absence of empathetic listeners, and isolation from celebratory moments of growth, can significantly deter spiritual progress. This means it is fundamentally important to cultivate and nurture meaningful connections. It is especially important to seek out supportive communities and actively participate in shared experiences that foster growth and healing. The journey of the soul through life is not a solitary pilgrimage; it is a shared odyssey, enriched by the connections we forge with others. Community acts as a crucial compass that guides individuals through challenging terrains, provides solace in moments of despair, and celebrates triumphs along the way. The shared spiritual journey, woven with threads of faith, struggle, and triumph, empowers individuals to navigate life's complexities with renewed resilience. The navigation also happens with compassion and a deeper sense of connection to themselves and the world around them. By actively engaging in community, we not only help others to grow, but also nurture our own spiritual development. We transform individual journeys that then become a collective testament to the enduring power of the human spirit. The symbiotic relationship between spiritual growth at the level of the individual, and the supportive context of community is a fundamental truth that transcends cultural and religious boundaries. It also underscores the innate human need for connection and shared meaning. The tapestry of life, therefore, is woven with the threads of individual experience, and the strong, supportive cords of human connection; hence creating a richer, more resilient, and more meaningful existence.

Cultivating Inner Peace: Practices for Spiritual Wellbeing

The previous section emphasized the crucial role of community in navigating life's challenges and fostering spiritual growth. However, the journey towards inner peace and spiritual well-being is not solely dependent on external support. It requires a concerted effort to self-cultivate and diligently tend to the inner garden of the soul.

This involves a range of practices designed to quiet the mind, cultivate self-awareness, and foster a deeper connection with one's inner self; and, ultimately, a transcendent reality.

One of the most widely practiced and extensively researched methods for cultivating inner peace is meditation. Meditation, in its various forms, involves training the mind to focus on a single point of attention, such as the breath, a mantra, or a visual image. The focused attention helps to quiet the incessant chatter of the mind and reduces stress, anxiety, and feelings of overwhelm. Regular meditation practice can significantly improve mental clarity, emotional regulation, and overall well-being. Studies have shown that meditation can alter the brain structure and function, hence strengthening areas associated with attention, self-awareness, and emotional processing.

The benefits of meditation are not merely psychological; they extend to the spiritual realm. By quieting the mind, meditation allows for a deeper connection with one's inner self. It also fosters a sense of stillness and presence. This inner stillness can be the gateway that helps experience a sense of transcendence, a connection to something larger than oneself. Different meditative traditions offer diverse approaches, each with their own unique emphasis and techniques.

For instance, Vipassanā meditation, which originates from the Buddhist tradition, emphasizes the cultivation of mindfulness, and awareness of the present moment. Meanwhile, Transcendental Meditation (TM) focuses on the use of a personalized mantra to quiet the mind and achieve a state of deep relaxation.

Prayer, another widely practiced spiritual discipline, offers a means of connecting with a higher power, or a transcendent reality. Prayers can take many forms. It can be a formal liturgical prayer, or spontaneous expression of gratitude, supplication, or praise. The act of prayer, irrespective of its form, can be a powerful tool that helps cultivate inner peace. It also helps connect with a source of strength and comfort. For many people, prayer serves as a conduit for communicating with a divine being, to express gratitude for blessings received. They also seek guidance in times of uncertainty, and solace in times of sorrow.

The effectiveness of prayer in fostering inner peace is linked to its capacity to shift perspective. When faced with adversity, you can rely on prayer to help reframe challenging circumstances and offer a sense of hope and perspective. The act of surrendering worries and anxieties to a higher power can be profoundly liberating. It frees individuals from the burden of excessive self-reliance and fosters a sense of trust and acceptance.

Further, the repetitive nature of liturgical prayer can induce a meditative state that fosters tranquility and inner calm.

Different religious traditions have distinct approaches to prayer, which reflect diverse beliefs and spiritual practices. From the chanted prayers of the monastic orders to the spontaneous expressions of faith found in charismatic traditions, the variety of prayer practices highlights the universality of the human need to connect with something greater than oneself.

Mindfulness, a practice rooted in Buddhist traditions but increasingly adopted in secular contexts, involves paying close attention to the present moment without judgment. Mindfulness cultivates an awareness of thoughts, feelings, and bodily sensations, without getting carried away by them. This non-judgmental awareness helps to reduce reactivity and emotional distress and fosters a sense of calm and equanimity. Mindfulness practices, such as mindful breathing, mindful walking, and body scans, cultivate present-moment awareness, and help to counteract the mind's tendency to wander into the past or future.

Mindfulness can be integrated into daily life, so that it transforms mundane activities into opportunities for spiritual practice. For instance, mindful eating involves paying close attention to the sensations of taste, texture, and smell, appreciating the nourishment received. Mindful walking involves focusing on the sensation generated when the feet meet the ground, the rhythm of breathing, and the surrounding environment. By cultivating mindfulness in daily activities, one cultivates a heightened sense of presence and appreciation for the present moment. This reduces stress and enhances overall well-being. The integration of mindfulness into daily life transforms ordinary experiences into avenues for spiritual growth and enhances one's capacity for mindful interaction with the world.

Self-reflection is a crucial component of the spiritual journey. It involves setting aside time for introspection, examining one's thoughts, feelings, and behaviors, and exploring their underlying causes. Journaling can be a powerful tool for self-reflection, as it allows individuals to externalize their thoughts and feelings. It also helps them gain clarity on their inner world. Regular self-reflection allows one to identify patterns of thinking and behavior that might be contributing to unhappiness or stress; hence one can develop appropriate strategies to help cultivate more positive patterns. This process of self-discovery is essential for growth and transformation.

Self-care is inextricably linked to self-reflection and the cultivation of inner peace, and involves prioritization of activities that support physical, emotional, and spiritual well-being. Self-care might include exercising regularly, eating a healthy diet, getting sufficient sleep, cultivating meaningful relationships, and engaging in activities that bring joy and fulfillment. It does not mean self-indulgence; rather, a necessary investment in one's own well-being. It means creating a foundation for personal growth and spiritual development. Neglecting self-care can lead to burnout, emotional exhaustion, and reduced capacity for spiritual practice.

The practices of meditation, prayer, mindfulness, self-reflection, and self-care are not mutually exclusive. On the contrary, they are interwoven aspects of a holistic approach to spiritual well-being. They share synergies, support and complement each other, and ultimately cultivate inner peace, enhance self-awareness, and foster a deeper connection with oneself. In the process, one experiences a transcendent reality. The cultivation of these practices is not a destination, but a continuous journey that requires patience, perseverance, and a commitment to self-improvement. The journey towards inner peace is a lifelong process, marked by moments of growth, setbacks, and renewed commitment. The commitment to these practices, however, yields immeasurable rewards in terms of enhanced well-being, resilience, and spiritual growth. The pursuit of inner peace, therefore, is not simply an escape from suffering, but a path towards a more authentic, meaningful, and fulfilling life. This path is paved with practices that nourish the soul, creating a sense of harmony within and a deeper connection to the world around us.

The journey may be challenging, but the rewards far outweigh the effort expended. By cultivating these practices with diligence, one unlocks the potential for profound personal transformation, and a life lived in harmony with one's inner self and the larger cosmos. The journey is personal, but the destination, a state of enduring peace and spiritual well-being, is universally sought and universally achievable.

The Nature of Faith: Trust and Belief in the Unseen

In the previous section we explored various practices that cultivate inner peace and enhance our connection to the self. However, for many, this inner journey is inextricably linked to a belief in something larger than themselves; a connection to the Divine, often expressed through faith. Faith, a concept central to numerous religious and spiritual traditions is not merely blind acceptance of ideas. It is a complex tapestry woven from trust, belief, and experience. To understand its nature, we must delve into its multifaceted dimensions.

At its core, faith involves a profound trust in something unseen; something that transcends empirical verification. This trust is not necessarily passive. Instead, it is an active engagement with the world and the unknown, and, as Kierkegaard famously described it, a leap of faith. This "leap" does not imply recklessness, but rather a willingness to embrace possibilities beyond the scope of immediate sensory experience. It is a commitment to a belief system, a set of values or worldview that informs one's understanding of reality and the individual's place within it. This trust can be directed towards a personal God, an impersonal cosmic force, or a set of spiritual principles. The object of faith varies across traditions, but the underlying dynamic of trust remains consistent. The element of belief within faith is equally significant. Belief, in this context, does not signify mere intellectual assent. Rather, it encompasses a deep conviction, an acceptance that transcends doubt. This belief can stem from various sources: personal experiences, teachings from religious leaders, textual interpretations, or reasoned philosophical arguments. However, it is essential to acknowledge that belief is not always static. It can evolve and mature throughout one's life, shaped by personal growth, new experiences, and intellectual inquiry. The process of faith is dynamic but not static. It involves constant negotiation between personal experience and the accepted framework of belief. Doubt, far from being antithetical to faith, can serve as a catalyst for deeper understanding, and a more profound commitment. Wrestling with doubts can lead to a more robust and nuanced faith.

Faith often manifests as a deep-seated conviction that there exists a divine being or a transcendent reality. This conviction might be accompanied by a belief that the Divine is actively involved in the world, influencing events, offering guidance, and answering prayers. The nature of this divine involvement is subject to diverse interpretations across different faiths, ranging from a personal God who interacts directly with individuals, to a more impersonal cosmic order that operates according to predetermined laws. However, the shared thread is the conviction that there is something beyond the material world, something that informs and shapes human existence.

The role of experience in faith is equally compelling. Many individuals trace their faith back to specific personal experiences of profound insight, inexplicable events, or encounters that seemed to defy rational explanation. These experiences, often described as mystical or numinous, serve as powerful confirmations of their beliefs. They also reinforce their trust and deepen their conviction, and while they are subjective and personal, they can also be profoundly transformative. They can provide a compelling foundation for a life centered on faith.

In philosophy, various perspectives attempt to illuminate the nature of faith. Some emphasize the rational foundations of faith, arguing that faith is not simply a matter of blind belief, but can be supported by reasoned argumentation and philosophical reflection.

Others contend that faith is fundamentally a matter of personal conviction that transcends the realm of rational proof or disproof.

Still, others highlight the social and cultural dimensions of faith, suggesting that it is shaped and sustained through community, shared rituals, and the transmission of traditions across generations.

These diverse perspectives highlight the complexity of faith and underscore the fact that it cannot be easily reduced to a single definition or explanation.

The psychological dimensions of faith are also crucial. Studies have shown that faith can provide individuals with a sense of meaning, purpose, and hope. This can be particularly significant during times of suffering, loss, or uncertainty, as it becomes a source of comfort, resilience, and inner strength. The sense of belonging provided by religious communities can further reinforce the psychological benefits of faith - fostering social support and reducing feelings of isolation. Conversely, it is important to acknowledge that faith can also be a source of conflict and division, particularly when differing beliefs lead to intolerance or violence.

Throughout history, faith has played a pivotal role in shaping human societies and cultures. It has inspired acts of great compassion and selflessness, as well as acts of profound cruelty and intolerance. To understand this paradoxical nature of faith, we need to examine its complex interaction with power structures, social norms, and individual experiences. Faith has been used to justify both acts of remarkable generosity and acts of horrific violence. This highlights the importance of critical engagement with religious and spiritual beliefs. It does not imply a rejection of faith, but rather a call to reflect thoughtfully on its potential for both good and evil.

The relationship between faith and reason has been a subject of ongoing debate throughout history. Some theologians and philosophers argue that faith and reason are mutually exclusive, while others posit that they can coexist and complement each other. The former perspective suggests that faith transcends the realm of rational inquiry and operates on a different plane of understanding. The latter viewpoint suggests that reason can provide a framework for interpreting and understanding religious beliefs, as faith provides a motivational force to inspire action and commitment. This ongoing dialogue emphasizes the importance of engaging with both faith and reason in a critical and constructive manner.

Examining the varied expressions of faith across different religious traditions sheds light on its multifaceted nature. From the contemplative practices of Buddhism to the passionate devotion of Christianity, the rigorous ethical codes of Judaism and the mystical traditions of Sufism, the religions of the world offer a vast array of approaches to faith. These diverse traditions, which often differ in their doctrines and practices, also share a common thread: a profound yearning for connection with something beyond the self. Within that is a quest for meaning, purpose, and ultimate truth.

In conclusion, faith, far from being a monolithic concept, is a rich and multifaceted phenomenon shaped by trust, belief, experience, and a wide range of theological and philosophical perspectives.

To understand its nature, we need to delve into the diverse expressions of faith across different cultures and traditions and proceed to examine its psychological dimensions as we explore its historical and social contexts. Ultimately, faith is a profound personal journey, deeply interwoven with human experience as individuals seek meaning, purpose, and connection in a world often characterized by uncertainty and ambiguity. The power of faith lies in providing comfort and solace, as well as inspiring individuals to lead lives of purpose, compassion, and commitment to a higher ideal. Therefore, the ongoing exploration of faith remains a vital endeavor, which is crucial if we are to understand the human condition and our relationship to the Divine. This exploration is a journey of constant questioning, evolving belief, and a continuing search for meaning and connection.

Experiencing the Divine: Personal Encounters and Revelations

Experiencing the Divine often transcends the realm of intellectual understanding and enters the territory of profound personal encounters. These experiences, while subjective and incapable of empirical proof, form the bedrock of faith for countless individuals. They are moments of intense connection, feelings of overwhelming presence, or profound shifts in perspective, which leave an indelible mark on the individual's life. The nature of these experiences varies greatly and reflects the diversity of religious and spiritual traditions. It also reflects the unique personalities of those who encounter them.

For some, the experience may be a sudden and overwhelming revelation, a moment of clarity or epiphany that dramatically alters their worldview. This could involve a powerful sense of divine presence, a feeling of being utterly encompassed by love or grace, or a deep understanding of one's purpose and place in the universe. Such experiences often leave the individual with a sense of awe and wonder; a profound conviction of the reality of the divine.

These moments can be transformative, leading to a complete reorientation of life's priorities and values. The individual might feel called to a life of service, dedicated to expressing their gratitude for the experience. Such life-altering encounters can be potent catalysts for profound personal growth and spiritual development.

Others may describe their experience of the Divine as a more gradual unfolding, a progressive deepening of their connection to something larger than themselves. This might involve a gradual increase in awareness of how interconnected all things are, a growing sense of peace and tranquility, or a deepening empathy and compassion towards others. These experiences may not be characterized by singular, dramatic, moments, but rather by a subtle, yet persistent, sense of presence or gentle guidance; or an enduring feeling of being loved and supported. These gradual transformations can be equally profound, and lead to a subtle, yet powerful, shift in the individual's sense of self and their relationship with the world.

This slow burn of spiritual growth can be just as impactful as a singular overwhelming experience.

Descriptions of these encounters often utilize evocative and metaphorical language, and this reflects the limitations of human language in capturing the inexpressible. Individuals may describe feeling "overwhelmed with grace," "bathed in light," "touched by the hand of God," or "united with the Divine." These metaphors attempt to convey the intensity and ineffability of the experience, highlighting the limits of rational explanation and the importance of personal interpretation. The language used is always deeply personal, and reflective of the individual's cultural and religious background. Comparison of experiences across cultures reveals the universal, yet deeply personal, nature of these encounters.

The impact of these experiences extends far beyond the moment of occurrence. They often serve as a foundation for enduring faith and provide a source of strength, comfort, and guidance throughout life's challenges. When faced with adversity, the individual can draw upon the memory of these experiences, which remind them of the divine presence and support. This can be especially significant during times of grief, loss, or uncertainty. Such memories offer a lifeline in times of despair, serving as a testament to the enduring power of faith, and the enduring power of divine connection.

It's crucial to acknowledge the subjective and personal nature of these experiences. What one individual describes as a profound encounter with the Divine, another might attribute it to psychological factors, physiological states, or coincidences. There is no universally accepted method for validating or invalidating these experiences, as they are inherently personal and interior. Besides, they are deeply personal and shape the individual's belief system uniquely. Their significance lies in their subjective impact on the individual's life, and not in their objective verifiability.

Different religious and spiritual traditions offer various frameworks to help understand and interpret these experiences. For example, within mystical traditions, these encounters are often viewed as a direct experience of the Divine, a glimpse into the ultimate reality beyond the limitations of the material world. In other traditions, they may be interpreted as moments of divine grace, blessings, or prayers. The framework used shapes how individuals process and incorporate the experience into their belief systems. How one understands the experience influences the way they approach their faith and integrate it into their lives.

Culture and one's personal background are equally important in shaping the interpretation of these experiences. Cultural narratives, religious teachings, and personal upbringing influence how individuals understand and articulate their encounters.

They may interpret these experiences in line with their existing beliefs, or, alternatively, find themselves reassessing the beliefs and worldviews they previously held after considering these encounters. The framework of their cultural context shapes the experience and makes it intrinsically unique to them.

Furthermore, as one explores their personal experiences of the Divine. important questions arise about the nature of faith itself. Are these experiences the foundation of faith, or do they simply confirm pre-existing beliefs? Can faith exist without such personal encounters, and vice versa? Owing to these questions, one may wish to explore further as they challenge our understanding of belief, doubt, and relationship between humans and the Divine. The answers are deeply personal, and they reflect individual experiences and beliefs.

The questions highlight the complex interplay between reason, experience, and faith. And while rational inquiry can provide frameworks for understanding the world, personal experiences of the Divine often transcend rational explanation. They suggest a realm of understanding that extends beyond the bounds of empirical evidence. The integration of personal experience with rational inquiry is a fundamental aspect of the human spiritual journey, and the challenge lies in navigating the balance between the two. This continuous process of integration shapes the individual's spiritual and personal growth.

Finally, it is essential to approach the topic of personal experiences of the Divine with sensitivity and respect. These experiences are deeply personal, and they often hold immense significance for the individuals concerned. It is paramount to avoid judgment or skepticism, and to recognize the limitations of any external frameworks imposed on these inherently subjective events. It is crucial to adopt an attitude of openness and understanding, if we are to have a productive dialogue and respectful engagement about the diverse ways individuals connect with the Divine. Embracing diversity and understanding individual experiences is key to appreciating the richness and complexity of the human spiritual journey. Respectful understanding is at the core of constructive discourse on spiritual experiences.

The Power of Prayer
Communication with the Divine

Prayer, in its myriad forms, stands as a testament to humanity's enduring desire to connect with something beyond the tangible. It transcends the confines of organized religion and permeates diverse spiritual and cultural landscapes. From the hushed whisper of private supplication to the fervent chanting of a congregational liturgy, prayer offers a pathway for individuals to express their hopes, fears, gratitude, and lamentations to a perceived higher power. This communication, however ethereal it may seem, holds profound significance in shaping and individual's faith and fostering a sense of connection with the Divine.

The act of prayer itself is multifaceted. It is not merely the recitation of pre-written texts or the adherence to established rituals, although these undoubtedly play a role in many faith traditions. Rather, prayer encompasses a spectrum of interactions with the Divine, from formal and structured devotions to spontaneous and heartfelt expressions. Some individuals find solace in structured prayer, finding comfort in the familiar rhythm and cadence of liturgical prayers or the repetitive chanting of mantras. The structure provides a framework that helps them focus on their thoughts and emotions and allows them to center themselves in a space of contemplation and communion.

For others, the essence of prayer lies in the spontaneous outpouring of the heart, a direct and unfiltered dialogue with the Divine. These moments may arise in periods of intense emotion –overwhelming joy, profound grief, or pressing anxieties. These spontaneous expressions may help the individual release pent-up feelings, and experience a sense of being heard and understood, as well as a renewed sense of hope and resilience. The unstructured nature of such prayer allows for a unique level of intimacy and vulnerability.

Prayer takes varied forms just as the beliefs and cultures that nurture it. In many Abrahamic traditions, prayer often involves petitionary requests – asking for divine intervention in specific situations, such as healing, guidance, or protection. These prayers may be characterized by a sense of supplication, a humble plea for assistance from a benevolent power. In other traditions, prayer takes the form of adoration and praise, expressing profound gratitude and reverence for the Divine. These expressions may involve hymns, chants, or poetic pronouncements, all aimed at celebrating the glory and majesty of the Divine.

Contemplative prayer, prevalent in various mystical traditions, offers a different approach. It involves a process of silent reflection and meditation, aimed at cultivating a deeper awareness of the divine presence within and beyond. This form of prayer may not involve explicit requests or pronouncements, but rather a quiet attentiveness to the divine's presence, a silent communion that transcends words and thoughts. The focus lies on cultivating a state of inner peace and spiritual awareness.

Regardless of the form it takes, the power of prayer often lies in its transformative capacity. The act of prayer, even in the absence of perceived divine intervention, can be a powerful tool for self-reflection, emotional processing, and spiritual growth. The act of articulating one's thoughts and feelings, whether to a perceived deity or to oneself, can provide clarity, perspective, and a sense of inner peace. The discipline of regular prayer can cultivate habits of mindfulness, gratitude, and empathy, fostering personal growth and a deeper connection with one's own inner self.

The psychological benefits of prayer are well-documented. Studies have shown that prayer can reduce stress, anxiety, and depression, promoting feelings of well-being and resilience. The sense of connection with a higher power, the belief that one is supported and guided, can provide a source of comfort and strength during times of adversity. This sense of support can be particularly crucial during periods of grief, loss, or uncertainty.

The sociological impact of prayer is equally significant. Prayer often serves as a unifying force within communities, bringing individuals together in shared worship and devotion. Collective prayer can foster a sense of belonging, mutual support, and shared identity. It can strengthen community bonds and promote social cohesion.

The shared experience of prayer can transcend individual differences and create a space for unity and solidarity.

However, the notion of the efficacy of prayer remains a complex and often debated topic. The question of whether prayers are answered or whether they simply provide psychological comfort has been explored extensively. Empirical evidence on the effectiveness of prayer in achieving tangible outcomes is often inconclusive and frequently contested. Some studies have suggested a correlation between prayer and improved health outcomes, while others have found no significant effect. The inherent difficulty in measuring the effects of prayer, coupled with the diversity of prayer practices and beliefs, makes it a challenge to conduct definitive scientific studies.

This lack of definitive empirical evidence does not diminish the importance of prayer in the lives of many believers. For them, the value of prayer transcends the realm of measurable outcomes. The act of prayer itself, the process of communicating with the Divine, can be deeply meaningful and transformative. It can also foster spiritual growth and a sense of connection with something larger than oneself. The subjective experience of prayer, the feeling of being heard, understood, and supported, is often more significant than any measurable outcome.

The power of prayer, therefore, extends beyond the realm of empirical evidence and scientific validation. It resides in its profound ability to nurture faith, cultivate spiritual growth, and foster a sense of connection with the Divine. It provides a space for introspection, emotional processing, and development of spiritual resilience. Whether viewed as a means of direct communication with a higher power, or as a practice of self reflection and emotional regulation, prayer continues to hold an important place in the lives of countless individuals across diverse cultures and faith traditions.

The diverse interpretations and practices surrounding prayer highlight the richness and complexity of the human spiritual experience. The act of prayer, in all its forms, is a powerful testament to our inherent search for meaning, purpose, and connection. It reveals the enduring human need to reach beyond the confines of the material world and to engage with something larger than us. This yearning for transcendence, this desire to connect with the Divine It is a fundamental aspect of the human condition, and prayer serves as a potent expression of this deep-seated need. Ultimately, the significance of prayer lies not in its measurable outcomes, but in its profound capacity to shape individual faith, foster spiritual growth, and strengthen the human connection to the Divine. This is a continuing conversation, a journey of faith that unfolds uniquely for everyone. And it is this very personal and evolving nature of prayer that underscores its enduring power, and its essential role in the human spiritual landscape. The search for meaning and connection with the Divine is an ongoing human endeavor, and prayer offers a pathway to engage with that search. It also shapes both our individual journeys and the fabric of our communities.

Religious Rituals and Practices: Expressions of Faith

Religious rituals and practices form the bedrock of many faith traditions and serve as tangible expressions of deeply held beliefs and values. They are not mere symbolic gestures but active engagements with the Divine. They shape individual spirituality and foster a sense of collective identity. The diversity of these rituals reflects the vast tapestry of human religious experience, from the elaborate ceremonies of ancient temples to the intimate practices performed in private spaces. One must acknowledge the multifaceted nature of the rituals, if they are to understand them. This means acknowledging their social, psychological, and spiritual dimensions, which are interwoven to create a rich and complex fabric of faith.

One of the primary functions of religious rituals is to establish a structured pathway to the Divine. Many traditions incorporate formalized prayers, chants, or incantations, to provide a framework for focused devotion and communication with a higher power. The repetitive nature of some rituals, such as the chanting of mantras in Hinduism or the recitation of the rosary in Catholicism, can induce a meditative state. This can, in turn, foster inner peace and a sense of connection with the Divine. The rhythm and structure of these practices help to quiet the mind and allows for a deeper engagement with a spiritual experience. The act of participating in these rituals, even if initially rote, can gradually transform into a deeply personal and meaningful experience.

The role of religious rituals goes beyond serving the individual and acts as a crucial social function. They bring people together and create a shared sense of community and belonging. Collective worship, such as attending mass, participating in a Sabbath service, or engaging in communal prayer, reinforces social bonds, and fosters a sense of collective identity. These shared experiences transcend individual differences and create a sense of unity and solidarity within the group. The rituals themselves often involve specific social interactions – greetings, sharing of food, or communal acts of service. These serve to reinforce the social fabric of the community.

The social aspect of rituals is particularly significant in smaller, more isolated communities. In such settings, religious rituals can play a vital role in maintaining social cohesion and providing a framework for social interaction. They can also transmit cultural values and beliefs across generations. The shared rituals become a powerful way to affirm communal identity, strengthen social bonds, and perpetuate the cultural heritage of the group. They often serve as markers of significant life events, such as births, marriages, and deaths, and shape the collective experience of the community. They also provide support during times of joy and sorrow.

The psychological impact of religious rituals is profound. They provide a framework for managing life's challenges, offering comfort, solace, and a sense of meaning in the face of adversity. The rituals can function as coping mechanisms, providing a sense of control and predictability in situations where individuals feel powerless. They offer a space for emotional processing, and allow individuals to express their feelings of grief, joy, or anxiety; all within a safe and supportive environment. The ritualized expression of emotions can be therapeutic. It can also provide a release of pent-up feelings and facilitate emotional healing.

Furthermore, religious rituals often involve actions that are symbolic, which represent deeper spiritual meanings. For example, the washing of hands or feet in some traditions symbolizes purification and cleansing, the significance being both physical and spiritual renewal. Similarly, the lighting of candles can represent hope, illumination, or the presence of the Divine. The symbolic language of rituals enriches spiritual experience and creates a multi-layered meaning; and this meaning resonates with participants on different levels. The interpretation of these symbols may vary across individuals and cultures, and this adds another layer to the richness and complexity of the ritual.

However, the relationship between religious rituals and the belief of an individual is not always straightforward. Some individuals may significantly derive faith from participating in rituals, and have their spiritual beliefs reinforced. Such participation may also foster a deeper sense of connection with the Divine. However, for other individuals, the rituals might feel obligatory or even meaningless. They may view such rituals as primarily significant within their social function or their cultural significance. An individual's experience of a given ritual can be significantly shaped by their level of faith and personal interpretation of the ritual's symbolism, and the social context within which it is performed.

The evolution of religious rituals throughout history is a testament to the dynamic nature of faith and belief. Rituals often adapt and evolve to reflect changing social, cultural, and political contexts.

They maintain core elements even as they frequently incorporate new ones and sometimes reinterpret existing practices in response to changing societal needs and spiritual understandings. The continued adaptation of rituals reflects the living nature of faith, and demonstrates its capacity to respond to the ever-evolving human experience.

The study of religious rituals and practices provides crucial insights into how humans relate with the Divine. It also highlights the fundamental human need for meaning and purpose. The practices are not mere historical relics, but vital elements of contemporary religious life, and they provide both individual and collective pathways to engage with the spiritual realm. Their capacity to create community, provide emotional support, and offer a sense of meaning, underscores their enduring importance in human experience. The continued exploration of these rituals promises further understanding of the profound interconnectedness between faith, belief, and the shared human journey. Analyzing religious rituals through anthropological, sociological, and theological lenses reveals their multifaceted impact, and shapes individual lives as well as the broader social fabric.

The role of religious artifacts and spaces also contributes significantly to the richness of ritual practice. Sacred objects, like crosses, prayer beads, and religious texts, serve as focal points for prayer, meditation, and contemplation. In the process, they facilitate a deeper engagement with Divine. The physical spaces dedicated to religious practice, such as churches, mosques, and temples, are designed to create an atmosphere conducive to worship and spiritual reflection. The architecture, art, and music within these spaces evoke a sense of awe, reverence, and connection, and this enhances the overall ritual experience. These spaces frequently serve as anchors for the community, foster a sense of belonging, and promote social cohesion.

Moreover, the transmission of religious knowledge and practices across generations through rituals maintains the continuity of religious tradition. Many rituals are passed down through families and communities, preserving cultural heritage and transmitting religious beliefs and values across time. This intergenerational transmission of knowledge ensures that religious traditions continue to thrive and evolve, as they adapt to changing cultural landscapes. The ritual itself becomes a form of pedagogy that teaches religious doctrine, and imparts social values, ethics, and ways of interacting with the world.

The ongoing study of religious rituals and practices allows for a deeper appreciation of the rich tapestry of human spiritual experience. By understanding the historical, social, and individual dimensions of these practices, we gain a broader perspective on the role of religion in shaping human lives and communities across time and cultures. The multifaceted nature of rituals—as social binders, psychological support, and spiritual pathways—demonstrates their enduring power and influence on human societies. Ultimately, the study of these rituals helps to illuminate the profound and enduring human search for meaning, connection, and transcendence.

Doubt and Faith: Reconciling Conflicting Beliefs

The preceding discussion highlighted the multifaceted nature of religious rituals and their profound impact on individual and collective life. However, the journey of faith is not always smooth or unwavering. Doubt, a seemingly contradictory force, often emerges as a significant challenge in the human relationship with the Divine. This section delves into the complex interplay between doubt and faith and explores how individuals navigate moments of uncertainty as they reconcile conflicting beliefs and maintain, or even deepen, their connection to what they perceive as sacred.

Although doubt is not at all the antithesis of faith, it can, in certain contexts, act as a catalyst for spiritual growth. It necessitates a re-examination of beliefs, and forces individuals to confront their assumptions as they engage in a more profound understanding of their faith. The absence of doubt might indicate a passive, uncritical acceptance of dogma, which hinders true spiritual engagement.

Conversely, the experience of doubt encourages a more active and conscious participation in one's faith. It also compels individuals to critically evaluate their beliefs and seek deeper meaning. This process of questioning, which entails wrestling with uncertainty, can lead to stronger and more resilient faith.

This dynamic is not unique to any specific religious tradition. Individuals encounter moments of doubt across the spectrum of faith experiences, whether one is involved deeply in personal reflection as with a solitary contemplative, or in the vibrant communal worship of a large congregation. The devout Christian may grapple with the problem of evil, questioning the omnipotence and benevolence of God in the face of suffering. The practicing Muslim might find themselves questioning specific interpretations of the Islamic law or struggling with reconciling tradition with modernity. Similarly, a committed Buddhist might encounter moments of skepticism regarding the nature of reality. or the efficacy of meditation practices. Doubt, in its various forms, is an intrinsic part of the human spiritual journey.

The sources of doubt are as diverse as the individuals who experience them. Meanwhile, intellectual challenges that arise from scientific discoveries or philosophical arguments can undermine established beliefs. Personal experiences, such as profound loss or suffering, can erode faith in a benevolent or just divine power. Exposure to conflicting religious viewpoints or cultural perspectives can sow seeds of uncertainty. Further, internal conflicts that arise from personal struggles with morality, ethics, or self-doubt, can cast doubt upon one's spiritual convictions. These internal and external pressures frequently intertwine and create a complex tapestry of challenges to faith.

Navigating these turbulent waters requires a nuanced and multifaceted approach. Many find solace and strength in engaging in their religious community. As they share doubts and vulnerabilities with fellow believers, participate in communal rituals, and receive spiritual guidance from religious leaders, they feel comforted and supported. The shared experience of doubt within a supportive community often strengthens bonds and fosters a sense of collective resilience.

Moreover, many find that intellectual engagement strengthens their faith. Studying theology, philosophy, or religious history can provide frameworks within which to understand and address their doubts. Also, individuals can broaden their perspectives and deepen their understanding by exploring diverse interpretations of religious texts and engaging in thoughtful dialogue with others who hold different beliefs. Rather than viewing intellectual inquiry as a threat to faith, they approach it as a tool for strengthening their belief system.

The role of personal experience cannot be overlooked. While doubt can arise from personal suffering, it is also in the depths of adversity that many individuals find their faith renewed and reinforced. Confronting hardship and finding meaning and purpose amidst pain can deepen their spiritual connection. This process frequently entails grappling with profound questions of existence, suffering, and justice, and ultimately leads to a more mature and complex understanding of their faith.

The process of reconciling conflicting beliefs often involves a revision of one's understanding of faith itself. For some people, this might mean adopting a more nuanced or liberal interpretation of their religious doctrine. For others, it might necessitate a complete shift in their belief system. Regardless of the outcome, the process of grappling with doubt promotes intellectual and spiritual growth. It is through this process of self-reflection and critical analysis that individuals often arrive at a more authentic and deep personal understanding of their relationship with the Divine.

Therefore, the journey of faith is not a passive acceptance of dogma, but a dynamic and ongoing process of engagement, questioning, and reconciliation. It is a journey characterized by moments of unwavering certainty and others of profound doubt. The very act of wrestling with doubt, of confronting uncertainty, often leads to a deeper and more meaningful connection with the divine. This process of critical engagement where we seek understanding in the face of adversity ultimately strengthens our human spirit and deepens our appreciation for the complexities of faith.

It is crucial to recognize that the resolution of doubt is not always a neat and tidy process. Some individuals may find that their doubts persist, leading to a change or abandonment of their faith. Others may find that their doubts eventually subside, leading to a renewed sense of faith and certainty. Still others may find themselves navigating a lifelong of tension between faith and doubt, where they keep constantly reevaluating their beliefs and adjusting their understanding of the Divine. The trajectory of this journey is unique to every individual.

Furthermore, it is vital to acknowledge the diversity of experiences related to doubt and faith, and the fact that there is no single "right" way to navigate this internal conflict. What works for one individual may not work for another. What is essential is commitment to genuine self-reflection, and the willingness to engage with both the comforting aspects of faith and the challenging aspects of doubt. This ongoing process fosters spiritual maturity and leads to a more profound and nuanced understanding of oneself and one's relationship with the transcendent.

The exploration of doubt and faith necessitates an examination of the very nature of belief. Belief is not simply a matter of intellectual assent, but a deeply personal, and often emotional, commitment. It involves trust, hope, and a willingness to embrace the unknown.

Doubt, then, can be seen as a challenge to this trust and hope, as it requires a reassessment of one's commitment. This reassessment, however challenging, can ultimately lead to a stronger and more authentic faith. The journey of faith is a lifelong exploration, a continuous process of learning, questioning, and refining one's understanding of the Divine and one's place within the cosmos.

Doubt, then, becomes not an enemy of faith but a crucial companion on this ongoing journey. It is in the wrestling with doubt that faith often finds its truest and most profound expression.

The tension between these seemingly opposing forces fosters growth, nuance, and a deeper, more resonant connection with the spiritual realm. This dynamic process allows for a more mature and resilient faith, one that can weather the storms of life and emerge stronger and more resilient than before. The acceptance of this inherent tension is, therefore, not just a coping mechanism, but a cornerstone of a genuinely lived faith.

Heaven and Hell: Exploring Traditional Concepts

The exploration of the afterlife inevitably leads us to consider enduring, if often contrasting, concepts of heaven and hell. These destinations, which represent ultimate reward and ultimate punishment, have captivated human imagination for millennia. They have shaped religious beliefs, ethical frameworks, and personal aspirations across diverse cultures and faiths. While the specifics vary dramatically depending on the religious or philosophical tradition, the fundamental dichotomy—a positive realm of bliss versus a negative realm of suffering—remains a persistent theme in humanity's contemplation of what lies beyond mortal existence.

In Abrahamic religions—Judaism, Christianity, and Islam—the concepts of heaven and hell are intricately woven into their theological narratives. Judaism, while not explicitly detailing a heaven and hell in the same manner as later traditions, envisions a world to come (Olam Ha-Ba) characterized by divine judgment and reward based on one's deeds in this life. This judgment, while not always presented as a literal fiery hell, often implies a state of spiritual separation from God for those who will have strayed from the divine law. The righteous, on the other hand, anticipate a life of closeness to God and the restoration of the world.

Christianity, which draws significantly from Jewish traditions, develops these concepts further. The New Testament introduces the idea of a heavenly kingdom, a realm of eternal bliss in the presence of God; as contrasted with the concept of hell, which is a place of eternal torment and separation from God. This vision is often interpreted allegorically, where it symbolizes the ultimate spiritual consequences of one's choices; an interpretation that many Christians take literally. The nature of hell's suffering, whether physical or spiritual, has been debated extensively throughout Christian history, with some theologians emphasizing its severity and others suggesting possibilities of purification or even ultimate reconciliation.

Islam, similarly, presents a vision of an afterlife that encompasses both paradise (Jannah) and hell (Jahannam). Paradise is depicted as a garden of unimaginable beauty and delight, while hell is characterized by fire and intense suffering. However, Islamic theology, also emphasizes the mercy of God and the possibility of forgiveness. This suggests that hell might not be an eternal state for everyone who has committed sin. The concept of divine justice, combined with the possibility of repentance and redemption, remains central to the Islamic understanding of the afterlife.

Beyond Abrahamic faiths, a vast range of perspectives on the afterlife exists. In ancient Egyptian religion, for instance, the journey into the afterlife involved a complex process of judgment and transformation. In this religion, the deceased's fate was said to be determined by their actions when they were alive, and their ability to navigate the underworld. The concept of reincarnation features prominently in many Eastern religious and philosophical traditions, which include Hinduism, Buddhism, and Jainism. These belief systems often envision a cyclical process of death and rebirth, where the soul transmigrates to different forms of existence based on its karma; karma being the accumulated effect of one's actions. There is no single, fixed "heaven" or "hell" in these systems, but rather a continuous process of striving for spiritual liberation (moksha) or enlightenment (nirvana).

In Buddhist thought, the concepts of heaven and hell are not necessarily permanent destinations but temporary states of existence within the cycle of samsara. Deeds performed in this life influence one's next rebirth. Therefore, one has the potential to lead to a pleasurable existence in a heavenly realm or a painful existence in a hellish realm. Nevertheless, neither is ultimate nor permanent. The goal is to break free from this cycle entirely and to achieve nirvana, which is– a state of liberation from suffering and the cycle of rebirth.

Hinduism presents a similarly complex view. It features a multitude of heavens and hells, each corresponding to different levels of spiritual attainment or transgression. The goal, again, is moksha, which is liberation from the cycle of birth, death, and rebirth, which transcends the limitations of both heaven and hell. The concept of karma plays a crucial role in determining the soul's journey through these various realms.

Philosophical viewpoints beyond religious frameworks also offer perspectives on the afterlife, and they often challenge or reinterpret traditional concepts. Some philosophical perspectives suggest that death is simply the end of consciousness, while others propose different possibilities. Among the suggested possibilities is the subsequent survival of the soul in some form, or the continuation of consciousness in a different plane of existence. These views often engage with the question of personal identity and explore the aspects of the self that might persist beyond physical death.

It is of paramount importance that we consider the nature of consciousness itself, if we are to understand these diverse perspectives. What constitutes "self" or "soul" is fundamental to the very understanding of an afterlife. Does the "self" consist solely of the physical body and brain, or is there a non-physical element that persists after death? This question has been debated for centuries by philosophers and theologians alike, and the varied conclusions arrived at influence the various interpretations of heaven and hell. The dualistic model that separates mind and body, readily lends itself to the belief that the soul endures and transcends physical death. Meanwhile, monistic viewpoints tend to view consciousness as a product of the brain, thus ending with bodily death.

The role of divine justice is another critical aspect in understanding the concepts of heaven and hell. The idea of rewards and punishments in the afterlife often reflects a belief in a just and morally ordered universe. However, the ways in which this justice is understood and implemented vary greatly across different traditions. Some traditions emphasize retributive justice, where the suffering is proportionate to one's wrongdoing, while others focus on restorative justice that aims for the rehabilitation and redemption of the soul.

Furthermore, the varying depictions of heaven and hell reveal a great deal about the cultural and social values of the communities that hold these beliefs. Descriptions of heaven often reflect the desires and aspirations of the culture. For example, paradise is depicted differently in different places and in different times. This demonstrates that values might have changed over time. Similarly, the descriptions of hell usually reflect that community's greatest fears and anxieties. For example, the threat of fire and brimstone in Abrahamic traditions reflects concerns around destruction and divine wrath. Meanwhile, other cultures might highlight different fears.

Throughout history, art, literature, and music have profoundly shaped our understanding of heaven and hell and have rendered these abstract concepts more tangible and accessible. There are paintings depicting the glorious landscapes of paradise or the terrifying torments of hell, literary works portraying the journeys of souls through the afterlife, and musical compositions evoking the emotional intensity of both realms. All these artistic expressions have greatly influenced our collective imagination and perceptions.

In conclusion, the concepts of heaven and hell, while appearing straightforward at first glance, reveal an extraordinary depth and complexity when examined across various religious, philosophical, and cultural contexts. Their variations illustrate the multifaceted ways in which humanity has grappled with the profound questions of life, death, and the ultimate destiny of the soul.

The exploration of these concepts continues to be a significant undertaking, which has necessitated continued reevaluation and fostering of dialogues across disciplines. Ultimately, the meaning and significance of these concepts remain deeply personal, shaped by individual beliefs, experiences, and the ever-evolving relationship between humanity and the transcendent.

Whether understood literally or metaphorically, the concepts of heaven and hell retain their power to inspire hope and fear. They also inspire a persistent quest for meaning and purpose in the face of mortality.

Reincarnation and Rebirth: Cyclical Views of the Souls Journey

The exploration of heaven and hell as realms of ultimate reward and punishment provides a stark contrast to the cyclical view of the soul's journey found in many Eastern traditions. Instead of a single, definitive destination after death, these perspectives posit a continuous cycle of birth, death, and rebirth; a process often described as reincarnation or transmigration. This cyclical model fundamentally alters our understanding of the soul's destiny and shifts the focus from a final judgment to an ongoing process of growth and transformation.

Central to the concept of reincarnation is the idea of karma. In Hinduism, Buddhism, Jainism, and other related belief systems, karma represents the cumulative effect of one's actions, thoughts, and intentions. These actions generate karmic imprints that influence subsequent rebirths. Good deeds and virtuous intentions lead to favorable rebirths, perhaps in higher realms of existence or in more fortunate circumstances. Conversely, negative actions and harmful intentions result in less desirable rebirths, potentially in lower realms or with increased suffering. This intricate system of karmic consequence shapes the soul's journey across lifetimes. Essentially, it drives the soul's ongoing evolution and strives for its spiritual liberation.

The concept of reincarnation isn't simply about repeating the cycle of life and death indefinitely. Instead, it's understood as a process of spiritual development. Each rebirth provides an opportunity for learning, growth, and the gradual refinement of one's karma.

Through repeated cycles, the soul gradually progresses towards a higher state of being, ultimately striving for liberation from the cycle of samsara—the continuous cycle of birth, death, and rebirth—itself. This liberation, often referred to as moksha in Hinduism or nirvana in Buddhism, signifies the transcendence of the limitations of the physical world and the attainment of a state of ultimate peace, enlightenment, and freedom from suffering.

In Hinduism, the concept of reincarnation is deeply intertwined with the notion of atman—the eternal, unchanging self—and Brahman—the ultimate reality or cosmic principle. The atman, often described as a spark of the divine within everyone, is believed to transmigrate from one life to another, ultimately aiming to reunite with Brahman. The journey towards this union is long and arduous, and it involves various rebirths in different forms of existence as influenced by one's karma. Hindu scriptures, such as the Bhagavad Gita, describe the cycle of reincarnation and the path to liberation in detail, emphasizing the importance of dharma (righteous conduct) and the pursuit of spiritual knowledge (jnana).

The specific details of the process can be intricate, with multiple levels of existence, heavens, and hells. They also include different forms of rebirth, all contributing to the complexity of this cosmological model. The path towards moksha is often portrayed as a challenging but ultimately rewarding journey of self-discovery and spiritual growth.

Different schools of Hindu thought may offer slightly varying interpretations of the process, but the overarching theme of cyclical existence and the pursuit of liberation remains consistent.

Although Buddhism shares some similarities with Hinduism, it offers a distinct perspective in its understanding of karma and reincarnation. Instead of an eternal, unchanging soul (atman), Buddhism emphasizes the concept of anatta (no-self), which suggests the individual self is a temporary construct, an ever-changing aggregation of physical and mental elements. While there is a continuity of consciousness across rebirths, there is no permanent, independent entity that transmigrates. The process of rebirth is governed by karma, but the goal is not the union with a divine being but the attainment of nirvana, a state of liberation from suffering and the cycle of samsara. This liberation involves the extinction of craving, attachment, and ignorance, which leads to the cessation of suffering and the end of rebirth. The Buddhist path to nirvana emphasizes ethical conduct, meditation, and the development of wisdom, all aimed at extinguishing the causes of suffering and achievement of lasting peace. The Buddhist understanding of heaven and hell differ from Abrahamic traditions, as these states are not eternal but temporary. Within the cycle of samsara, they reflect the karmic consequences of one's actions in previous lives.

Jainism, a tradition closely related to Hinduism and Buddhism, presents a similar cyclical view of the soul's journey. Like Buddhism, it rejects the concept of an eternal, unchanging self. Instead, it emphasizes the liberation of the soul (jiva) from the cycle of reincarnation, through the practice of ahimsa (non-violence), tapas (self-discipline), and other spiritual practices.

The goal in Jainism is to achieve liberation (moksha), a state of complete freedom from the cycle of birth and death, where the soul transcends the limitations of the material world. The concept of karma in Jainism is particularly nuanced, with different types of karma influencing the soul's experiences in its various rebirths. The emphasis on non-violence stems from the belief that all living beings, regardless of their form, possess a soul, and harming any of them creates negative karma, which then prolongs the cycle of reincarnation.

The cyclical views of the soul's journey, as found in these traditions, offer a compelling alternative to linear models of the afterlife. These perspectives emphasize the ongoing process of spiritual development. They also emphasize the importance of karmic consequences and the goal of liberation from the cycle of birth, death, and rebirth. While the specific details vary across the different traditions, the overarching theme of continuous striving, evolution, and pursuit of spiritual freedom remains a powerful and influential concept in shaping the spiritual understanding of countless individuals worldwide.

These cyclical models also raise fascinating questions about personal identity and the nature of consciousness. If the self is not a fixed entity but rather a constantly evolving stream of consciousness, what is it that carries over from one lifetime to the next? How do memories, experiences, and personal characteristics persist across rebirths? These are questions that have been debated extensively within these traditions, and various philosophical approaches offer different interpretations. Some suggest a subtle continuity of consciousness, a sort of karmic imprint that influences future lives. Others focus on the continuous flow of consciousness, with each rebirth representing a new phase of experience that is connected but not identical to previous incarnations.

Furthermore, the understanding of karma and reincarnation raises ethical considerations. The idea that one's actions have long-term consequences, extending beyond this life, have profound implications on how we live and interact with the world. It encourages ethical conduct, compassion, and a commitment to positive action, not only for the benefit of others in this life but also for the betterment of one's future rebirths. This emphasis on ethical action creates a system of accountability that extends beyond earthly justice. It also fosters a sense of responsibility that impacts one's actions on the wider world, and the continuity of one's spiritual journey. The cyclical models underscore the interconnectedness of all beings, and the importance of acting in ways that promote harmony and well-being for all.

The concept of reincarnation, therefore, is more than just a belief about the afterlife. It is a profound worldview that shapes ethical frameworks, personal aspirations, and the understanding of the self and its place in the universe. It encourages a long-term perspective and emphasizes the significance of each action. It also emphasizes the importance of striving for spiritual growth and liberation throughout the continuous journey of existence. It underscores the inherent interconnectedness of life and reminds us that our actions in this life have far-reaching consequences, influencing not only our present reality but also the course of our future rebirths. The ongoing examination of these cyclical views provides a unique and insightful perspective on the complexities of existence and the ultimate destiny of the soul.

The Souls Transformation: Progression Beyond Physical Existence

The cyclical models of the afterlife, prevalent in Eastern traditions, offer a compelling alternative to the linear, judgment-based narratives of Western religions. Instead of a singular destination –heaven or hell – these perspectives posit a continuous process of growth and transformation, where the soul's journey transcends the confines of a single lifetime. This progression, however, is not a passive or automatic process. Rather, it is one actively shaped by the individual's actions, intentions, and spiritual practice. The concept of karma acts as a dynamic force, driving the soul's evolution across multiple lifetimes.

One crucial aspect to consider is the nature of the soul itself. While Western traditions often conceive the soul to be an unchanging essence, many Eastern philosophies portray it as a more fluid entity that is constantly evolving and adapting through experience. In Buddhism, for instance, the concept of anatta (no-self) rejects the notion of a permanent, independent soul. Instead, it suggests that what we perceive as self is a constantly changing aggregation of physical and mental factors. This does not negate the continuity of experience across rebirths, but it reframes our understanding of personal identity.

The individual's consciousness, experiences, and karmic imprints carry over, yet the precise configuration of "self" is in constant flux.

This evolving concept of self presents a fascinating challenge to the idea of a soul's "transformation." If the self is not a fixed entity, what, precisely, undergoes transformation? The answer, arguably, lies in the gradual refinement of karmic imprints, and the diminishing of attachments and desires that bind the soul to the cycle of samsara. Each rebirth provides opportunities to learn, grow, and address the karmic consequences of past actions. Through conscious choices and spiritual practice, the individual can progressively purify their karma and weaken the ties that perpetuate suffering and the cycle of rebirth.

This purification is not a mere reduction of negative karma, but a growth in spiritual awareness and compassion. The accumulation of positive karma contributes to more favorable rebirths, but the goal transcends such relative improvements. The aim in both Buddhism and Jainism is nirvana or moksha —a state of liberation from the cycle itself. This is the state where the individual transcends the limitations of the material world and attains a state of profound peace and enlightenment.

In Hinduism, the concept of atman —the eternal self—adds another layer to the understanding of transformation. While the atman is considered eternal and unchanging, its experiences across multiple lifetimes shape its evolution towards union with Brahman, the ultimate reality. The journey is not about a change in the atman's essence, but a realization of its inherent unity with Brahman. This process involves a gradual unfolding of the atman's true nature, through the shedding of illusion and the attainment of self-knowledge.

The different paths to liberation, which comprise the various yogic practices in Hinduism, the eightfold path in Buddhism, and the emphasis on ahimsa (non-violence) in Jainism, all aim to facilitate this process of transformation. These practices provide tools to cultivate inner peace, overcome attachments, refine karma, and ultimately achieve a state of liberation. Meditation, ethical conduct, selfless service, and the pursuit of wisdom, are crucial elements in this process of spiritual evolution.

Consider the metaphor of a sculptor who refines a statue from a rough block of stone. The stone itself remains the same, but the sculptor's skillful work gradually reveals its inherent beauty and form.

Similarly, the soul, or atman, remains constant, but through the process of karmic refinement and spiritual practice, its inherent potential for enlightenment gradually unfolds. Each lifetime represents a phase in this process, a step closer to the goal.

Furthermore, the concept of realms of existence, both positive and negative, within these cyclical models, does not represent a static, destination but rather a set of temporary states within the larger cycle of rebirth. These realms, often described as heavens and hells, reflect the karmic consequences of actions and intentions. However, they are not permanent and the soul's residence within them is also temporary. The soul's duration within the different realms is determined by the extent of its karma. Even within these realms, opportunities for spiritual growth and transformation exist. Therefore, there is a chance for karmic refinement even in seemingly less favorable circumstances.

In these cyclical models, the idea of progress is not a linear ascent towards a singular point of perfection. It is a multifaceted process of refinement, purification, and liberation. Progression is not measured by accumulating heavenly rewards but by the gradual reduction of suffering, elimination of negative karmic imprints, and awakening of inner wisdom and compassion. This transformative journey emphasizes the long-term consequences of one's actions, and the profound impact conscious choices have on the soul's trajectory throughout its multiple lifetimes.

The specific mechanisms of how this transformation occur remain a subject of ongoing debate and interpretation within these religious and philosophical traditions. Some suggest a process of subtle imprinting of karmic energy on the soul, which influences its future rebirths. Others focus on the continuity of consciousness and put emphasis on the gradual accumulation of wisdom and compassion that shape the soul's experiences and motivations. Regardless of the specific mechanism, the common thread is the emphasis on a continuous, evolutionary process, driven by karma and shaped by the individual's choices and spiritual practices.

The emphasis on the interconnectedness of all beings within these cyclical models also influences the nature of the soul's transformation. The concept of karma highlights the repercussions of actions. not only on oneself but on others. A focus on compassion, non-violence, and ethical conduct arises from the recognition of this interconnectedness. One must also recognize that actions ripple outward and affect the entire cosmic order even as they influence future rebirths. The soul's transformation, therefore, is not solely an individual journey, but a process interwoven with the destinies of others.

The exploration of the soul's transformation after physical death presents a profoundly complex and multifaceted issue. While the details and specific mechanisms may vary across different traditions, the overarching theme remains: the soul's journey being a continuous process of evolution, shaped by karma, intention, and conscious choices. This process transcends the limitations of a single lifetime, encompasses multiple rebirths, and culminates in the attainment of liberation from the cycle of suffering and rebirth itself. The nature of this transformation, whether it is gradual refinement of a fixed entity or an evolving stream of consciousness, highlights the enduring power of spiritual practice and the long-term consequences of our actions in shaping the soul's destiny. This ongoing exploration encourages a deeper understanding of the afterlife as well as a more mindful and purposeful approach to life itself. The pursuit of spiritual growth, ethical conduct, and compassion becomes not merely a path to a future reward, but a vital part of the soul's continuous transformation, its ongoing journey toward liberation.

Eternal Life and Immortality: Concepts of Enduring Existence

The previous discussion centered on cyclical models of the afterlife and highlighted the continuous evolution of the soul through repeated lifetimes. Let us now delve into the contrasting, yet equally compelling, concept of eternal life and immortality—the notion of an enduring existence beyond the cyclical nature of birth and death.

This concept, while sharing some common ground with cyclical models, presents a distinctly different perspective on the soul's destiny. It often emphasizes a singular, permanent state, rather than a continuous process of transformation.

The idea of eternal life, often associated with Western religious traditions, typically envisions a state of permanent existence after death. This state could be either in a heavenly realm or a state of blissful union with the Divine. This idea differs significantly from the Eastern religious traditions, which place emphasis on liberation from the cycle of rebirth. In Christianity, for instance, the promise of eternal life is a central tenet. It promises believers a life of unending joy and communion with God in Heaven, a state often depicted as a perfect and unchanging paradise. This promise of a reward beyond the confines of mortality serves as a powerful motivator for ethical conduct and spiritual growth during one's earthly life. The concept of judgment, too, which entails determination of an individual's ultimate destiny, is a significant element within this framework. It highlights the importance of faith, good work, and adherence to divine commandments.

However, the concept of "eternal life" itself is open to varying interpretations. Some people understand it as a continuation of personal consciousness, essentially an eternal "self" existing in a transformed state. Others posit a more mystical union with the Divine, where an individual's identity may be subsumed within a greater cosmic consciousness. The debate around the precise nature of eternal life—whether it involves the preservation of a distinct individual self or a merger into a larger, transcendent reality—has been a central theme in theological and philosophical discourse for centuries. This has led to diverse interpretations and beliefs within Christianity and other faiths that promise eternal life.

Judaism still posits a concept of an afterlife and ongoing existence of the soul, although it does not explicitly detail a heaven or hell in the same way as Christianity. The emphasis is often on the continuity of the soul, and its connection to God, although the specifics of this existence remain less defined than in some other traditions. Members are encouraged to live righteous lives in accordance with God's commandments, and expect a future reward linked to this earthly existence. The concept of resurrection, both physical and spiritual, is also a significant theme, which implies a form of eternal life that transcends simple continuation of the soul's existence.

Islam shares similarities with both Judaism and Christianity regarding eternal life. The Quran describes a day of judgment where individuals will be judged for their deeds and assigned to either Paradise (Jannah) or Hell

(Jahannam). Paradise is depicted as a realm of eternal bliss, while Hell represents eternal punishment. The emphasis is heavy on individual accountability, the consequences of actions, and the importance of adherence to Allah's will. The belief in resurrection plays a vital role, where the soul is expected to be reunited with the body on judgment day; that is before it ultimately enters either Paradise or Hell for eternity.

The concept of immortality in certain philosophical schools of thought takes a different path from that taken by the Abrahamic religions, whose perspectives are largely linear, and judgment focused. Consider the Stoic philosophers of ancient Greece and Rome, who viewed immortality as a form of enduring influence on the world through one's actions and contributions, as opposed to a continuation of personal existence in a heavenly realm. For them, true immortality is achieved through the lasting impact one has on society, the ethical principles one embodies, and the wisdom one imparts, and not through an afterlife. Their focus on virtues and living in accordance with nature, offered a path to a form of immortality that transcends the limitations of physical death.

Similarly, some schools of thought within secular humanism view immortality as the legacy one leaves behind—the impact of one's work, ideas, and relationships on future generations. This approach avoids the supernatural entirely and focuses on the lasting contributions individuals make to the world. It also focuses on the ongoing influence individuals exert even after their physical death. This notion of immortality is grounded in the tangible and measurable, and emphasizes the power of human action in shaping the course of history; also, to inspire future generations. The focus shifts from a transcendental afterlife to an enduring influence in the temporal world.

The tension between cyclical and linear models of the afterlife raises fundamental questions about the nature of self, consciousness, and the very meaning of existence. If the soul is constantly evolving and transforming, as suggested by cyclical models, what does it mean to achieve true immortality? Does immortality necessitate the preservation of a fixed, unchanging self, or does it exist within a state of continuous change and growth? The concept of eternal life, as presented by many Western religions, seems to imply a static, unchanging state of existence, while cyclical models suggest a dynamic, ever-evolving process.

This difference highlights the inherent limitations of any human attempt to define or comprehend the afterlife. Our understanding of death, the soul, and the nature of reality is inherently limited by our earthly experience. The various perspectives presented – the linear narratives of eternal life and the cyclical journeys of reincarnation – are not necessarily mutually exclusive. They may represent different facets of a larger, more complex reality that transcends our current capacity for complete understanding.

Moreover, the pursuit of understanding the afterlife often influences how we live our lives. The promise of eternal reward or the fear of eternal punishment can significantly impact moral choices and spiritual practices. Alternatively, the understanding of a continuous cycle of rebirth might emphasize compassionate action and the pursuit of spiritual liberation. Regardless of one's specific belief system, the contemplation of one's destiny after death inevitably raises existential questions about the meaning of life, the importance of moral action, and the ultimate nature of reality. This contemplation provides a valuable framework within which to reflect on our place in the world; also, on how we can best contribute to the ongoing nature of humanity.

The philosophical implications of eternal life and immortality extend beyond the purely religious. The question of enduring existence has profoundly influenced ethical systems, political ideologies, and artistic expressions throughout history. The belief in a future judgment has informed the development of moral codes, legal systems, and artistic representations of heaven and hell. Conversely, the emphasis on a cyclical view of existence has often led to different cultural values and priorities, such as the importance of living ethically in the present moment and preparing for future rebirths.

Ultimately, the concepts of eternal life and immortality remain central to human experience. They offer both comfort and challenge, as they inspire hope, fear, and a profound sense of wonder.

The diverse perspectives and ongoing debates around these concepts, demonstrate the enduring power of the human spirit to grapple with the fundamental questions of existence, meaning, and our place in the cosmos. The varied approaches to understanding the soul's destiny—whether a singular, eternal state, or a continuous process of transformation—enrich our exploration of what it means to be human, and to exist within the vast mystery of life and death.

The continued exploration of these concepts promises further insights into the intricacies of human consciousness, and our ongoing search for understanding the ultimate reality.

The Unknown Afterlife Exploring Uncertainty and Speculation

The preceding sections have explored various established belief systems regarding the soul's destiny and offered structured narratives of cyclical rebirth and linear progression towards eternal life.

However, the reality of death and what follows is still shrouded in profound uncertainty. While faith provides comfort and structure for many, the inherent incapacity to understand the afterlife leaves space for questioning, speculation, and the acceptance of ambiguity.

This section, therefore, ventures into the realm of the unknown, as we acknowledge the limitations of human understanding; also, as we acknowledge the diverse ways through which individuals grapple with the mystery of what lies beyond death.

The very notion of an "afterlife" implies a continuation of consciousness or existence in some form, after the cessation of biological life. But what form does this take? Owing to the lack of empirical evidence, it becomes necessary to rely on philosophical arguments, theological interpretations, and personal experiences, though often subjective and difficult to verify. Some might find solace in the narratives provided by religious traditions, finding structure and meaning in established doctrines. Others may find these narratives insufficient, or even incompatible with their own understanding of reality. Such individuals may, instead, prefer to embrace the incomprehensible nature of death.

One significant challenge in exploring the unknown afterlife is the inherent difficulty in defining consciousness itself. What constitutes "self"? Is it solely a function of the brain, which disappears entirely with the brain's demise, or is there a non-physical aspect that persists?

Materialist perspectives often lean towards the former, suggesting that consciousness is a product of complex neurological processes, and therefore ceases to exist upon the death of the body. However, numerous spiritual and religious traditions posit the existence of a soul or spirit, a non-physical entity that survives the death of the physical body. Hence, it may continue to exist in some form.

The diverse range of near-death experiences further complicates the issue. Accounts of individuals experiencing out-of-body sensations, encounters with deceased loved ones, or perceptions of a transcendent reality, are frequently cited as evidence for a continued existence beyond death. However, the scientific community often interprets these experiences through the lens of neurological activity, brain chemistry, or psychological factors. Consequently, they emphasize the need for caution in trying to interpret these experiences as conclusive proof of an afterlife. The fact that interpretations vary dramatically highlights the subjectivity involved in interpreting such experiences, and the lack of a universally accepted framework within which to understand them.

Furthermore, the possibility of a non-physical reality, often posited by spiritual and religious belief systems, introduces further layers of complexity. Many belief systems suggest realms beyond our physical perception, dimensions, or planes of existence, where souls may reside after death. Descriptions of these realms vary drastically across different cultures and religions, ranging from the heavenly paradises of Abrahamic religions to the cyclical realms of rebirth in Eastern traditions. The very idea of a non-physical realm presents a significant challenge to our current scientific understanding of the universe, leaving individuals to rely more on faith, intuition, and interpretations of spiritual experiences.

The lack of definitive answers regarding the afterlife also makes it necessary to consider different approaches in trying to deal with mortality. Some individuals might find comfort in faith-based beliefs, which offer solace and hope amidst the uncertainty. Others may find solace from a secular perspective, whose focus is on the impact of their lives in the world and the legacy they leave behind. Still, others may choose to embrace the ambiguity and accept the incomprehensible nature of death; meanwhile focusing on living a meaningful life in the present. Each approach reflects a different way of navigating the inherent mystery of existence and confronting the limitations of human knowledge.

In considering the incomprehensible aspects of the afterlife, we can also acknowledge the role of culture and personal experience. Cultural narratives and beliefs deeply shape an individual's approach to death and the concept of an afterlife. Beliefs about the soul, the significance of life events, and the nature of the world beyond death, are often deeply ingrained in cultural practices, rituals, and traditions. These cultural factors often play a crucial role in shaping personal beliefs and influencing how individuals cope with their mortality and that of loved ones. Understanding these cultural influences can help us appreciate the diverse ways people conceptualize the afterlife, and the varying levels of comfort and anxiety they associate with it.

The concept of the soul itself remains a subject of intense debate and diverse interpretations. Is the soul a singular, unified entity, or is it an entity that is fragmented and distributed throughout the body or the universe? Some traditions view the soul as a distinct entity that exists independently of the physical body. Other perspectives see it as interwoven with the body; meaning it ceases to exist once the body dies. Some even posit the soul as part of a larger cosmic consciousness, which loses its individual identity upon death. These differing perspectives underscore the vast spectrum of beliefs regarding the nature of the soul and its potential fate after death.

The inherent uncertainty of the afterlife also raises profound ethical considerations. If there is no discernible afterlife, how does that impact our moral choices and actions during our lives? The absence of an external judgment or reward system might lead some to question the significance of ethical behavior. Conversely, the understanding that our actions have a lasting impact on others and the world around us may further emphasize the importance of living ethically.

Ultimately, grappling with the unknown afterlife is an inherently human endeavor, which reflects our deepest fears and hopes regarding mortality. It invites us to engage in critical self-reflection, and to question our beliefs and assumptions about life, death, and the nature of existence. Embracing the uncertainty of the afterlife rather than seeking definitive answers, may ultimately encourage a greater appreciation for the present moment, and the value of human connection. The mystery remains, and perhaps, it is in this mystery that we find the most profound invitation to live fully, love deeply, and embrace the inherent wonder and beauty of human experience. This is regardless of what may, or may not, lie beyond. The exploration continues, for the unknown is not the absence of meaning, but the constant invitation to create meaning in the face of the vast expanse of the unanswered.

The Power of Choice: Shaping Our Own Destinies

Exploring the mysteries of the afterlife naturally leads us to a crucial consideration: the role of free will in shaping our individual destinies. If the afterlife exists, does it represent a predetermined path; a consequence of actions already ordained? Alternatively, is it a realm influenced and shaped by the choices we make in this life? This question intersects with fundamental philosophical and theological debates that have engaged thinkers for millennia. The concept of free will itself is a complex tapestry woven from threads of

determinism, libertarianism, and compatibilism, each offering a unique perspective on human agency and its power to alter our fate.

Determinism, a philosophical position with ancient roots, posits that all events, including our choices, are causally determined by prior events. In essence, our actions are predetermined. They are the inevitable outcomes of a chain reaction stretching back to the beginning of time. From this perspective, free will is an illusion, a subjective feeling of agency that masks the inexorable workings of causality.

This view has implications for the afterlife: If our choices are

predetermined, then our destiny in any potential afterlife is, likewise, predetermined. This leaves little room for individual agencies to shape our fate. Hard determinism, a more rigid version of this view, leaves no room for moral responsibility, as our actions are not truly our own. Conversely, soft determinism acknowledges the constraints of causality but still allows for a limited sense of free will. This suggests that our choices are made within parameters set by prior events.

Libertarianism, in contrast to determinism, champions the notion of genuine free will. It asserts that we possess the capacity to make choices that are not causally determined by prior events. This means we have genuine freedom to choose between different courses of action. Also, it implies a degree of self-causation, where our choices originate from within our own consciousness, unconstrained by external factors. In the context of the afterlife, libertarianism suggests that our choices in this life directly impact our fate in any potential hereafter. Ultimately, this makes us the architects of our own destiny. The actions we take, the relationships we forge, and the beliefs we adopt are not simply the result of fate, but deliberate choices that shape our spiritual journey.

Compatibilism, an attempt to bridge the gap between determinism and libertarianism, proposes that free will and determinism are not mutually exclusive. It argues that free will is compatible with determinism and suggests that if our actions are causally

determined, we still possess a degree of freedom if our choices are aligned with our desires and intentions. Our choices, while determined, are nevertheless genuinely ours, because they stem from our internal motivations and beliefs. If we apply this premise to the afterlife, it suggests that our choices, although ultimately determined, play a significant role in our post-mortem experience. They also reflect a predetermined path shaped by our freely chosen actions within a causal framework.

Theological perspectives on free will add another layer of complexity. Many religious traditions incorporate the concept of free will within their frameworks of salvation, damnation, or reincarnation. In Abrahamic religions, for instance, the notion of divine judgment emphasizes the significance of individual choices in determining one's eternal destiny. Good deeds, righteous living, and faith are often seen as crucial in securing a positive outcome in the afterlife. Conversely, actions deemed sinful or morally reprehensible may lead to negative consequences in the afterlife. This viewpoint underscores the profound responsibility inherent in the exercise of free will, as our choices have eternal repercussions.

Eastern religious traditions, such as Hinduism and Buddhism, often incorporate the concept of karma, which links actions and intentions to future consequences, including reincarnation. Karma suggests that our actions generate karmic energy, which determines our future lives. This is a cyclical process where our choices in one life influence our experiences in subsequent lives. This perspective underscores the long-term implications of free will and highlights the interconnectedness of present actions and future lives. Even in the absence of a definitive "afterlife" as understood in Western religions, the continued impact of our choices through the cycle of rebirth emphasizes the profound significance of conscious decision-making.

However, even within theological frameworks, questions regarding the extent and limits of free will persist. Is our free will absolute or is it constrained by divine providence? Does God's foreknowledge of our choices negate our free will? These are longstanding theological debates with no easy answers. The tension between divine sovereignty and human agency is a recurring theme in religious thought, and it reflects the complex interplay between predestination and individual responsibility. The answer often lies in the specific interpretation of religious texts and traditions, each offering unique perspectives on this fundamental conflict.

The implications of our choices extend beyond the theological realm and permeates various aspects of human existence. In ethics, for instance, the concept of free will forms the cornerstone of moral responsibility. If we lack free will, how can we be held accountable for our actions? If our choices are preordained, then the very concept of moral responsibility seems to unravel. This fuels the ongoing debate between moral responsibility and determinism, a debate that highlights the profound significance of the free will concept in our understanding of ethical behavior.

In psychology, the question of free will influences our understanding of human motivation and behavior. Do our internal drives, unconscious processes, or genetic predispositions entirely dictate our actions, or can we make a conscious choice to shape our behaviors? This question is central to many therapeutic approaches. Some of them focus on addressing underlying unconscious patterns, while others emphasize the power of conscious choice and self-determination. Understanding the degree of freedom, we possess in shaping our behaviors is crucial to personal growth and self-actualization.

The power of choice, therefore, is not simply a philosophical or theological abstraction, but a fundamental aspect of the human experience.

It affects how we understand our past, shape our present, and project our future. While the existence and nature of an afterlife remain shrouded in mystery, the impact of our choices during our mortal lives is undeniable. The choices we make, big or small, collectively shape our character, forge our relationships, and ultimately determine the legacy we leave behind in the world.

This inherent power of choice should not be underestimated. Even in the face of uncertainty, the potential to shape our own destiny, both in this life and possibly beyond, makes the conscious exercise of our free will an act of profound significance. The journey of life is not merely a pre-determined path; it is a dynamic narrative that we actively co-create with every choice we make. And in that co-creation, we discover the profound power and responsibility of human agency.

Moral Responsibility: Accountability for Our Actions

The preceding discussion of free will and its implications for various aspects of human existence naturally leads us to the crucial concept of moral responsibility. If we truly possess the capacity for free choice, as libertarianism suggests, or even a degree of freedom within a deterministic framework, as compatibilism proposes, then we must also grapple with the inherent accountability that accompanies such an agency. Moral responsibility, therefore, is not merely a philosophical abstraction, but a fundamental aspect of our ethical and social lives that shapes our relationships, communities, and understanding of justice.

The core principle of moral responsibility rests on the premise that individuals are accountable for their actions and their consequences. This accountability is not simply about-facing external repercussions, such as legal penalties or social ostracism, although these are certainly significant aspects. More fundamentally, moral responsibility involves an internal acknowledgment of our role in shaping the world around us. It encompasses an awareness of the impact our choices have on ourselves and others. This self-awareness is crucial and serves as the foundation upon which ethical behavior and a just society are built.

Consider, for instance, the act of lying. A deliberate falsehood, told with the intention to deceive, carries a moral weight. The consequences might be relatively minor, such as a bruised ego or a missed opportunity, but they could also be far more significant. For example, it could lead to broken trust, damaged relationships, or even legal ramifications. Regardless of the specific outcome, the act of lying itself represents a failure to exercise moral responsibility. The individual who chooses to lie has knowingly violated a fundamental ethical principle – the principle of honesty – and must therefore bear the consequences of that choice.

This concept extends far beyond simple actions like lying. It encompasses a vast spectrum of human behavior, including acts of kindness, generosity, compassion, and cruelty. Choosing to act with empathy towards those in need demonstrates a high degree of moral responsibility. It also reflects a commitment to ethical principles. a recognition of our interconnectedness. Conversely, acts of violence, hatred, and oppression represent a profound failure of moral responsibility. It indicates a disregard for the well-being of others, and a rejection of fundamental ethical obligations.

The question of moral responsibility, however, is not always straightforward. Several factors can complicate our assessment of an individual's accountability. Circumstances, for instance, can play a significant role. A person who acts under duress, coercion, or extreme emotional distress might be held less morally responsible for their actions than someone who acts freely and deliberately. Similarly, age and mental capacity can influence our assessment of moral responsibility. We generally hold children and individuals with severe mental illnesses to a lower standard of accountability than adults with full cognitive function.

Furthermore, the complexities of human motivation and intentionality often blur the lines of moral responsibility. An action that appears morally reprehensible on the surface might have been undertaken with good intentions, albeit with flawed judgment.

Conversely, an action that initially seems benign might reveal hidden motives, or unintended consequences that diminish its moral worth. These complexities highlight the challenges involved in trying to definitively assign moral responsibility. They also emphasize the importance of careful consideration, context, and empathy.

The concept of moral responsibility also has profound social and political implications. Our legal systems, for example, are largely built upon the principle of individual accountability. Criminal justice systems are designed to hold individuals responsible for their actions, while civil courts address disputes and conflicts based on the principle of individual liability. These systems, however, are not perfect, and the complexities of assigning responsibility often led to injustices and inequalities.

The challenge lies in navigating the nuances of individual agency within a complex social context. Factors, such as poverty, systemic inequality, and lack of opportunity can significantly influence an individual's choices and actions, hence creating a tension between personal and social responsibility. Addressing these challenges requires a holistic approach, which recognizes the interplay of individual choices and societal structures in shaping human behavior and its consequences.

Religious perspectives further enrich the understanding of moral responsibility. Many religious traditions emphasize the importance of accountability and connect individual actions to divine judgment or karmic consequences. In Abrahamic religions, for example, the notion of divine justice underscores the eternal implications of our choices and highlights the profound responsibility to live ethically and righteously. The concept of a divine reckoning, whether in the afterlife or during earthly life, reinforces the seriousness of moral responsibility, and the need to act with integrity and compassion.

Eastern religious traditions, such as Hinduism and Buddhism, offer a different lens through which to view moral responsibility – emphasis on the concept of karma. Actions and intentions, according to this perspective, have long-term consequences in this life as well as in subsequent lives that emerge through reincarnation. Karma underscores the interconnectedness of our actions and their repercussions, and highlights the importance of conscious, ethical decision-making. The cycle of birth, death, and rebirth provides a framework within which to understand the continuous impact of our choices. It emphasizes the far-reaching implications of moral responsibility.

However, the question of whether moral responsibility is compatible with a deterministic worldview remains a subject of intense philosophical debate. If all events, including our choices, are predetermined, as hard determinism suggests, then how can we be held accountable for our actions? If our choices are simply the inevitable outcome of a chain of prior events, then the very concept of moral responsibility seems to unravel. This debate highlights the fundamental tension between free will and determinism, and their implications for ethics and justice.

Soft determinism attempts to bridge this gap by suggesting that free will and determinism are compatible. Our choices, even if casually determined, are still considered "free" if they are aligned with our desires and intentions. This perspective allows for a degree of moral responsibility even within a deterministic framework. It also acknowledges the complexities of human motivation, and the importance of aligning our actions with our values.

Ultimately, the concept of moral responsibility is not a matter of simple equations or definitive answers. It is a complex and multifaceted issue that requires careful consideration of various factors, which include free will, determinism, context, intentionality, and social influences. The ongoing exploration of moral responsibility is a vital aspect of human inquiry, which shapes our understanding of ethics, justice, and the very nature of human agency. It is a journey of constant self-reflection and ethical striving, a recognition of our profound accountability for the impact our choices have on ourselves, others, and the world around us. The implications of this responsibility, both personal and societal, are far-reaching, and they continue to shape our understanding of what it means to be human. It is a challenge that requires continuous engagement and thoughtful consideration, a testament to the depth and complexity of human experience.

Determinism vs Free Will: Exploring Competing Theories

The preceding discussion of moral responsibility naturally leads us to a fundamental philosophical divide: the age-old debate between determinism and free will. There is this seemingly simple dichotomy: Are our actions predetermined, or do we genuinely possess the power of choice? It has profound implications for how we understand ourselves, our relationships with others, and the very structure of our moral and legal systems.

Determinism, in its purest form, often called "hard determinism", posits that every event, including every human action, is causally determined by prior events. This means that our choices, like the movement of planets or the falling of rain, are merely links in an unbroken chain of cause and effect, which stretch back to the very beginning of time. In this view, the illusion of free will is precisely that—an illusion.

We believe we are making choices, but our actions are predetermined by factors beyond our conscious control: factors like genetics, upbringing, environmental influences, and the totality of past experiences. A hard determinist might argue that even the seemingly spontaneous act of choosing between two options is the inevitable result of complex, interwoven factors operating at a subconscious level.

The implications of hard determinism for moral responsibility are stark. If our actions are predetermined, how can we be held accountable for them? If we are merely puppets on strings of causality, how can we be justifiably praised for our good deeds or punished for our misdeeds? This challenge to the foundation of our ethical and legal systems has led many people to outright reject hard determinism, as they find it incompatible with our deeply ingrained sense of personal agency and responsibility. Indeed, the very act of holding someone morally accountable—praising or blaming them—implies the existence of free will; capacity to make a different choice.

However, the rejection of hard determinism does not necessarily mean that one must embrace Libertarianism without qualifying it. Libertarianism holds the philosophical position that we possess complete free will, meaning we are not constrained by any deterministic forces. This philosophy argues that our choices are genuinely free. That means we could have made different choices than we did, as our actions are not simply the result of prior causes. This position affirms the intuitive sense that we are the authors of our own lives; that we possess genuine agency and are responsible for our choices. Yet even libertarianism faces significant challenges. It struggles to reconcile the apparent freedom of our choices with the observable regularity and predictability of human behavior. Moreover, it raises questions about the nature of causation itself—if our choices are truly uncaused, how can they be understood or explained?

Compatibilism, a middle ground between hard determinism and libertarianism, attempts to reconcile the apparent conflict between free will and determinism. Compatibilists argue that free will and determinism are not mutually exclusive; they can coexist. They maintain that our actions are indeed causally determined, but that this does not negate the reality of free will. Instead, they redefine "free will" to mean acting according to one's own desires and intentions, even if those desires and intentions are themselves casually determined. In essence, a compatibilist would argue that a choice is "free" if it is not coerced or constrained by external factors. It remains the case even if that choice is the inevitable outcome of internal states and prior events.

For example, consider a person who chooses to donate something to charity. A hard determinist might argue that this action was predetermined by a complex interplay of genetic predispositions, upbringing, and current circumstances. A libertarian would insist that the person genuinely chose to donate and could have just as easily chosen not to. A compatibilist would agree that the action was casually determined but would emphasize that the donation was nonetheless free because it was in accordance with the individual's own values and intentions. Basically, the person genuinely wanted to donate, and nothing forced or coerced them to do so.

The implications of compatibilism for moral responsibility are significant. It allows us to maintain a sense of accountability even within a deterministic framework. In the Compatibilist sense, we can still praise or blame individuals for their actions even if those actions were ultimately predetermined, if they were performed freely, without external coercion. This position provides a potential bridge between the seemingly irreconcilable positions of hard determinism and libertarianism. However, critics of compatibilism argue that it redefines "free will" in a way that renders it meaningless. If our desires and intentions are themselves casually determined, then the apparent freedom of acting on them becomes illusory.

The debate between determinism and free will extends beyond the realm of pure philosophy. It has profound implications for our legal and ethical systems. Our justice systems are predicated upon the assumption that individuals are responsible for their actions and should be held accountable for their consequences. But if hard determinism is true, the very concept of justice is thrown into question. If our actions are predetermined, how can we fairly punish criminals or justly reward those who act virtuously?

Compatibilism offers a potential solution by suggesting that accountability is possible even within a deterministic framework. This, however, remains a contentious concept, with debate about the nature of justice and the appropriate response to crime continuing. Nevertheless, we live in a world where casual determinism may hold sway.

This debate intersects with theological considerations, especially because many religious traditions grapple with the tension between divine omnipotence (God's all-powerful nature) and human free will. If God is omniscient and omnipotent, meaning He knows and controls every event, then how can humans truly possess free will? Some theological perspectives resolve this tension by suggesting that God's foreknowledge of our actions does not negate our freedom to choose. Others emphasize the importance of human agency within the framework of divine grace and providence.

The debate between determinism and free will remains one of the most enduring and challenging issues in philosophy. There is no single, universally accepted answer, and different philosophical perspectives offer compelling, yet often conflicting, arguments. The exploration of these competing theories not only illuminates our understanding of human nature, but also shapes our ethical frameworks, legal systems, and religious beliefs. The ongoing dialogue continues to refine our understanding of what it means to be responsible and moral. It also enhances our understanding of what it means to exercise an agency in a complex, and often unpredictable, world. The implications are vast. They reach into every facet of human experience and influence our understanding of personal responsibility, societal structures, and the nature of reality itself. Ultimately, the resolution, or even some form of satisfactory reconciliation, of this profound duality remains an open question; a persistent challenge for philosophers, theologians, and anyone seeking a deeper understanding of the human condition.

The Illusion of Choice: External Influences on Decision Making

The preceding exploration of determinism, libertarianism, and compatibilism sets the stage for a deeper examination of the complexities that surround free will. While the philosophical debate grapples with the ultimate source of agency, the reality of human decision-making is often far more nuanced, and less abstract than these grand theoretical frameworks suggest. This section delves into the practical limitations our perceived freedom of choice. We acknowledge the pervasive influence of external factors and internal biases, which subtly, and sometimes overtly, shape our decisions.

The notion of a completely autonomous, unfettered will, capable of making choices entirely independent of external influence, is arguably a utopian ideal. In the real world, our choices are constantly shaped and molded by a complex interplay of forces, from subtle social pressures to powerful environmental factors.

Consider the impact of socio-economic status on life choices. An individual born into poverty may have limited access to education, healthcare, and opportunities, and that would significantly restrict their range of options. The case is different for someone born into privilege. The circumstances of their birth, factors entirely outside their control, profoundly shape the trajectory of their lives, and the choices they can realistically make. This is not to say that such individuals lack freedom in entirety. Rather, their range of genuinely free choices is constrained by their environment. Their freedom is not absolute, but rather conditional, determined partially by factors outside their immediate control.

This principle extends beyond economic circumstances. Cultural norms and social pressures exert a powerful influence on our decision-making. The pressure to conform to societal expectations, such as career-related choices, marriage, or even religious beliefs, can significantly curtail the perceived freedom of individuals. In some societies, the social stigma associated with certain choices, such as a non-traditional career path, or expression of dissenting opinions, may lead individuals to suppress their true desires. Ultimately, they resign themselves to conforming to the dominant norms. This conformity, driven by fear of social ostracism or ridicule, represents a significant limitation on the exercise of free will. An individual might believe they are making a free choice, but their decision is, in fact, shaped and constrained by the fear of social consequences; such being fundamentally external factors.

In other instances, the pervasive influence of advertising and media significantly impacts our choices. The constant bombardment of marketing messages designed to manipulate our desires and shape our consumption patterns demonstrates a clear case of external influence on our decision-making. The subtle manipulation of emotions, the creation of artificial needs, and the promotion of specific lifestyles, all contribute to a landscape in which our choices are not entirely our own. We may believe we are choosing freely, but the options presented to us, and the desirability of those options, are carefully constructed and presented by external forces. Essentially, we have choices, but they are not presented on a level playing field. Rather, they are strategically curated to influence our decisions in a predetermined direction.

The impact of environmental factors is not limited to social and media influences. Physical and geographical limitations can also significantly impact our options. And individuals who live in a remote area with limited access to resources or opportunities fundamentally have restricted life choices, compared to one who lives in a densely populated urban center. Similarly, the prevalence of certain diseases or health conditions can severely restrict the life choices available to the affected individuals. These external environmental factors do not actively coerce an individual into making certain choices, but they undeniably influence the range and nature of options available to them. The free will of an individual who suffers from a debilitating illness is not the same as that of a healthy individual. Obviously, the range of plausible actions for the two varies dramatically.

Beyond external influences, our internal cognitive biases significantly affect our decision-making processes. Cognitive biases are systematic errors in thinking that can lead us into making irrational decisions, often against our own best interests. Confirmation bias, for instance, leads us to seek out and interpret information that confirms pre-existing beliefs, while ignoring contradictory evidence.

This bias can severely limit our capacity to make rational and objective choices. This is because we essentially filter information to support our pre-existing conclusions. Yet, the choice that is seemingly free is predicated upon a distorted perception of reality. Similarly, anchoring bias, whereby we overemphasize the first piece of information we receive, can lead to suboptimal choices. The reason is that we fixate on this initial anchor, rather than rationally evaluating all available options. These internal biases act as invisible constraints. They influence our decisions without our conscious awareness.

The phenomenon of choice architecture further highlights the limited scope of our free will. Choice architecture refers to the way choices are presented to us. It can influence our choices without any overt coercion. For example, the placement of items in a supermarket significantly affects the decisions we make regarding our purchases. When items are placed strategically at eye level, or near the store checkouts, it often leads to impulsive purchasing. Similarly, the phrasing of options on a ballot can influence voting patterns. These examples demonstrate how the framing of choices, a carefully constructed external factor, can subtly manipulate decision-making; meanwhile the individuals believe they are making free and independent choices. The illusion of choice is maintained, but the reality is a much more constrained range of effective choices.

Even our personal decisions that seem most private are subject to some subtle influences. Consider the profound impact our early childhood experiences have on our personality, beliefs, and values. Our upbringing, including our familial relationships, educational experiences, and peer interactions, shapes our perspectives and frames our understanding of the world. These early experiences, largely outside our control, often lay the foundation for future choices, even if we are unaware of their influence. Our adult choices, therefore, are not entirely independent, but deeply rooted in our past experiences. Some of the influencing experiences become effective before we even have the capacity for conscious decision-making.

The legal system, predicated on the notion of individual responsibility, implicitly acknowledges the complexities of free will.

While we are held accountable for our actions, mitigating circumstances, such as duress, coercion, or diminished capacity, are considered before determining culpability. These factors, which represent external constraints on free will, impact the severity of punishment, or even the determination of guilt or innocence. Recognition of such mitigating factors implicitly acknowledges that the concept of absolute free will is not realistic, regarding how we view human behavior and decision-making.

In conclusion, while the philosophical debate on free will continues to rage, the practical reality of human decision-making reveals a far more complex picture. Our choices are shaped and constrained by a multitude of external influences and internal biases, and this suggests that the ideal of a completely autonomous will is likely an unattainable notion. This does not negate the importance of personal responsibility or diminish the significance of individual agency.

Rather, it promotes a more nuanced understanding of the factors that contribute to our choices. It reminds us that the "illusion of choice" is often deeply embedded in the very fabric of our decision-making processes. Once we understand these influences, we can take a more compassionate and just approach to judging individuals and be more realistic in assessing the range and limitations of human freedom.

The challenge, then, is not to abandon the concept of free will entirely, but to engage with the complexities of human decision-making. We can accomplish this by accounting for the significant influences that shape our choices, without minimizing our capacity for moral responsibility. The interaction between internal agencies and external pressures provides a rich and complex field of study; one that continues to challenge and refine our understanding of what truly means to be human.

Embracing Freedom Cultivating Responsible Choice

Embracing the complexities of free will, as explored in the preceding sections, does not lead to nihilism or dismissal of personal responsibility. It only paves the way for a more profound understanding of the human condition, and a more nuanced approach to ethical decision-making. Acknowledging the myriads of influences that shape our choices empowers us to cultivate responsible agencies. It enables us to make conscious choices aligned with our values and aspirations. It requires a conscious effort to overcome biases, identify limiting factors, and develop strategies to help navigate the complex landscape of decision-making.

One crucial step in cultivating responsible choice is cultivating self-awareness. This involves a rigorous examination of our own cognitive biases, and how they might subtly, or not so subtly, distort our perception of reality and influence our choices. If we understand our predispositions to confirmation bias, for example, we can actively seek out dissenting viewpoints and challenge our pre-conceived notions. Once we recognize the influence of anchoring bias, we can strive to actively consider a wider range of options, so we can avoid the trap of fixating on the first piece of information we receive.

Regular self-reflection, journaling, or even mindfulness practices can assist in developing this crucial self-awareness. The practice of metacognition, which means thinking about our thinking, is invaluable in this process. By carefully examining the processes that lead to our decisions, we can begin to identify and mitigate the impact of our inherent biases.

Beyond individual biases, cultivating responsible choice demands a critical evaluation of the external forces that shape our options. We must strive to identify and understand the influence of social pressure, media messaging, and environmental limitations on our decision-making. This involves actively questioning the narratives presented to us, critically evaluating the information we consume, and actively seeking out diverse perspectives. This critical analysis extends to the subtle influences of choice architecture, and recognition that the framing of options significantly impacts our choices. By becoming more aware of how choices are presented, we can make more informed and less manipulated decisions. For instance, once we understand how strategically supermarkets place items, we may be able to resist impulsive purchases. Similarly, if we understand the framing of political discourse, we can approach political choices with greater critical discernment.

Furthermore, developing a strong ethical framework is essential for navigating the complexities of decision-making. This involves defining our core values and principles and clarifying our goals and aspirations. it also entails aligning our choices with these guiding principles.

This process may necessitate difficult choices and require us to prioritize certain values over others. For instance, an individual may value both financial security and social justice. However, a job offer that prioritizes profit over ethical labor practices would necessitate making a difficult choice; of balancing the competing values. A well-defined ethical framework provides a clear guide through which to navigate such dilemmas. Such a guide provides a moral compass to help navigate the complexities of human choice.

Another important aspect of responsible choice is cultivating emotional intelligence. Our emotions can significantly impact our decision-making and often override any rational considerations.

To develop emotional intelligence, one must learn to recognize and manage personal emotions. It is important to understand how emotions influence our choices and hence make decisions based on both reason and empathy. To succeed in this, one must self-regulate, be able to control impulses, and avoid making rash decisions - those driven by immediate emotional responses. One must also understand the emotions of others, practice empathy, and consider the impact their choices have on those around. Fostering emotional intelligence helps to make more thoughtful and considerate choices. In the process, we mitigate the risk of impulsive actions driven by unchecked emotions.

In addition to individual strategies, cultivating responsible choices requires engaging in the wider societal context. This involves advocating for policies and practices that promote equity and justice. Such fairness ensures that everyone has access to the resources and opportunities needed to make informed choices. It is crucial to address systemic inequalities, such as those related to socio-economic status, access to education, and healthcare, in order to foster a society where individual agency is not unduly constrained by external factors. This engagement might involve participating in community initiatives, advocating for social change, or supporting organizations that work towards creating a more just and equitable world. By recognizing the interconnectedness of individual choices and societal structures, we can actively work towards creating a world where everyone has a fair chance to exercise their freedom of choice.

The cultivation of responsible choice is not a passive endeavor, but an ongoing process of self-reflection, critical analysis, and ethical engagement. It requires constant vigilance in identifying and mitigating biases, understanding external influences, and developing a strong ethical framework. It demands emotional intelligence and a commitment to social justice. The journey towards responsible choice is not about achieving perfect autonomy, a state arguably impossible to attain given the

complexities of human existence, but rather about striving to make conscious choices aligned with our values and goals; also, to a commitment to create a more just and compassionate world. This journey is about recognizing the limitations of our freedom, while simultaneously embracing the responsibility that accompanies it. It is a continuous process of learning, adapting, and evolving, as we navigate the multifaceted landscape of human experience. The pursuit of responsible choice is a lifelong journey of self-discovery and ethical engagement, a continuous striving for a more authentic and meaningful existence.

Furthermore, the concept of responsible choice extends beyond individual actions, to encompass our collective responsibility. The decisions we make as individuals have ripple effects, which impact not only ourselves and our immediate communities, but also the wider world. It is imperative that we consider the broader consequences of our actions if we are to engage in responsible decision-making. For example, the choice to consume products from companies with unethical labor practices has far-reaching consequences, which contribute to exploitation and injustice.

Similarly, the choice to ignore environmental concerns can have devastating long-term impacts on the planet and future generations.

Cultivating a sense of collective responsibility encourages us to consider the interconnectedness of our actions and to strive to make choices that benefit not only ourselves but also the wider community; and also, the environment.

The development of responsible choice also requires a deep engagement with the philosophical underpinnings of free will. The complexities of determinism and libertarianism may seem abstract, but if we understand these philosophical perspectives, we may be able to appreciate the nuances of human agency. Such comprehension challenges us to question the extent to which our choices are truly free, and to recognize the interplay between internal agency and external constraints. This awareness can lead to a more compassionate and considerate approach to ourselves and others. We would recognize that the path towards responsible choice is often fraught with challenges and complexities, and, therefore, approach decision-making with greater humility and a deeper understanding of the human condition.

Finally, the cultivation of responsible choice is a deeply personal and evolving process. What constitutes responsible choice varies depending on individual values, beliefs, and circumstances. There is no single formula or prescribed path for such determination. The journey towards responsible choice requires self-reflection, critical thinking, and a commitment to ongoing learning. It necessitates a willingness to confront our biases, question our assumptions, and embrace the complexities of human experience. It is a journey of continual growth and refinement, a process of becoming more conscious, compassionate, and responsible in our choices. In essence, the pursuit for responsible choice is a testament to the human capacity for self-awareness and moral reasoning. It is also a testament to the enduring quest for meaning and purpose, in a complex and often unpredictable world.

The Origins of Evil: Theological and Philosophical Perspectives

The exploration of responsible choice, as undertaken in the previous sections, naturally leads us to confront a profoundly challenging question: What is the origin of evil? Understanding the nature of evil is inextricably linked to our understanding of free will and agency. If we possess genuine freedom of choice, then how do we account for the pervasive presence of suffering, wickedness, and malevolence in the world? This question has haunted theologians and philosophers for millennia, generating a vast and complex body of thought. This section will delve into some of the key theological and philosophical perspectives on the origins of evil. These perspectives also acknowledge the limitations and inherent complexities of each approach.

One prominent theological perspective prevalent in many Abrahamic traditions attribute the origin of evil to a conscious act of rebellion against a benevolent God. This perspective, often articulated through the narrative of the Fall in Genesis, portrays evil to be a consequence of misused free will. Lucifer, or Satan, is depicted as a powerful angel, who, through pride and ambition, chose to defy God's authority. This narrative introduces sin and suffering into the world. It has a perspective that presents evil as a contingent reality, a product of a deliberate choice made by a created being, and not as an inherent force in the cosmos., While this explanation provides a seemingly clear origin of evil, it leaves unanswered questions pertaining to God's omniscience and omnipotence. If God knew Lucifer would rebel, why did He create him? And if God is omnipotent, why did He fail to prevent this act of rebellion? These questions have spurred centuries of theological debate, with some attempts being made to reconcile the existence of evil with God's attributes. Some theologians suggest that God permits evil to exist so that genuine free will can manifest., They argue that a world without the possibility of choosing evil would not be a world of true freedom. Others emphasize the concept of divine sovereignty. These ones argue that even within the context of free will, God ultimately orchestrates all events according to his divine plan. However, these responses do not satisfy some people, who raise questions about the compatibility of free will, divine foreknowledge, and divine power.

Another theological perspective offers a different understanding of evil's origin. This perspective, often found within certain strands of mystical thought, suggests that evil is not a positive force, but rather a privation of good, meaning an absence or deficiency of something inherently positive. This is sometimes referred to as "negative theology." In this view, evil does not exist independently, but only in relation to good. For example, darkness is not a substance but simply the absence of light. Similarly, evil is not a substance or entity but a lack of goodness; a distortion or corruption of what is inherently good. This approach addresses the problem of a powerful evil being pitted against an even more powerful God. However, it runs the risk of downplaying the seemingly real and destructive effects of evil actions. The suffering caused by human cruelty, for instance, feels very real, and is hardly a mere absence of good. It is a tangible, profoundly negative experience.

Philosophical perspectives on the origins of evil also offer diverse explanations. Some philosophers draw on deterministic views and suggest that evil is not a matter of choice but a consequence of causal chains operating beyond individual control. This perspective emphasizes the influence of genetics, environment, and societal structures in shaping human behavior. Evil actions, in this view, are not necessarily freely chosen, but determined by factors outside the individual's direct influence. However, this perspective faces challenges related to moral responsibility. If our actions are predetermined, can we truly be held morally accountable for them? Here, profound ethical implications arise, associated with concepts such as justice and punishment.

Other philosophical perspectives emphasize the role of human reason and knowledge in the origin of evil. Some people argue that the pursuit of knowledge, especially when divorced from ethical considerations, can lead to harmful consequences. The development of sophisticated weaponry, for instance, exemplifies the capacity for human ingenuity to be applied towards destructive ends. This suggests that the pursuit of knowledge, while valuable, requires ethical reflection and moral restraint to prevent its misuse. It also suggests a moral responsibility to integrate ethical considerations into all aspects of intellectual and scientific endeavors.

Furthermore, the potential for misuse of knowledge is exacerbated by human fallibility and biases. This highlights the need for continued ethical reflection, and development of mechanisms to safeguard against the misuse of knowledge.

Furthermore, the concept of evil is often explored through the lens of existentialism. Existentialist philosophers emphasize the inherent freedom and responsibility of human beings, which highlights the capacity for both good and evil to emerge from this freedom. Evil, in this perspective, is not an external force but a product of human choices; a manifestation of the absurdity and anguish of human existence. However, this perspective does not offer a clear explanation for the seemingly arbitrary nature of suffering and the disproportionate suffering innocent individuals experience.

The problem of evil highlights the challenge that persists in trying to reconcile the existence of suffering and wickedness with the belief in a benevolent God, or even the universe. This challenge persists whether we approach the problem from theological or philosophical perspectives. There are no easy answers, and each perspective offers its own strengths and limitations. The ongoing debate concerning the origins of evil serves as a testament to the enduring complexities of human existence, and the persistent quest for understanding the nature of good and evil; also, free will and determinism, and the intricate relationship between human agency and the larger cosmic order. The exploration of these perspectives fosters a deeper understanding of the human condition, and underscores the importance of cultivating both individual responsibility and compassion in addressing the pervasive presence of evil in the world. This understanding, in turn, informs and enriches our approach to responsible choice, and enables us to navigate the complexities of human action with a greater degree of wisdom and ethical awareness. Recognizing the inherent challenges and complexities that surround the origins of evil underscores the importance of a constant engagement with these questions and leads to a more nuanced and compassionate approach to ethical decision-making.

The seemingly irreconcilable nature of these perspectives underscores the profundity of the question. The various approaches that seek to explain the origin of evil provide a rich framework within which to explore the fundamental questions of human existence and our relationship with the divine or the cosmos. This is as opposed to offering definitive solutions. That framework highlights the need for continued intellectual and spiritual inquiry and encourages ongoing reflection on the nature of good and evil; also, on the limits of human understanding, and the importance of striving for a more just and compassionate world. This exploration, in turn, informs our understanding of responsible choice and prompts us to consider the far-reaching consequences of our actions; and the ethical imperative to mitigate suffering and promote the flourishing of all beings. The lack of a single, universally accepted answer is not a sign of failure, but a testament to the inherent complexity of the problem. It shows there is a need for ongoing dialogue and critical engagement. This constant questioning and re-evaluation are crucial for fostering a deeper understanding of the human condition and cultivating more responsible and compassionate choices.

The Problem of Evil: Reconciling Suffering with a Benevolent God

The problem of evil, the seemingly irreconcilable existence of suffering in a world governed by a benevolent and omnipotent God, has been a cornerstone of theological and philosophical debate for centuries. The sheer volume of human suffering—from natural disasters and disease to the horrors of war and intentional cruelty—presents a formidable challenge to traditional theistic beliefs. If God is all-powerful and all-good, why does He permit such widespread and intense suffering? This question has led to a multitude of responses, each with its own strengths and limitations.

One common response center around the concept of free will. The argument posits that God, in his infinite wisdom, granted humanity the gift of free will, the capacity to choose between good and evil.

This freedom, while essential for genuine moral agency and the experience of genuine love and devotion, inevitably carries the risk of choosing evil. The existence of evil, therefore, becomes not a failure of God's power or goodness, but a consequence of human choices. The suffering we witness is the result of human misuse of free will. Tragically, this freewill is necessary in this world where genuine love and commitment can flourish.

However, this perspective faces immediate and profound objections, the most obvious being the problem of innocent suffering. Why do infants, the mentally handicapped, or those who have spent lives of exemplary goodness suffer? Their actions, presumably, have not contributed to the suffering they endure. To attribute their suffering to their own choices seems morally reprehensible. This leads some people to modify the free will defense to suggest that God permits evil to facilitate the greater good of a world where genuine freedom exists, even if this freedom is occasionally exercised for malevolent purposes. The possibility of genuine love and moral growth necessitates the possibility of suffering and evil. God's ultimate purpose, then, might not be to eliminate suffering, but to allow the potential for true human flourishing, even amidst the challenges and sorrows of life. This understanding puts strong emphasis on the human capacity to establish meaning – finding meaning in our suffering and that of others.

Another approach focuses on the nature of God's omniscience and omnipotence. Some theologians argue that God's knowledge is not simply predictive; it transcends time. God sees the entire timeline of events, and this includes viewing all possible choices and corresponding consequences simultaneously. Thus, when God's permits evil, He is not guilty of failing to prevent it. Rather, He makes a deliberate decision based on His understanding of the ultimate good that is bound to emerge from allowing free will to operate. This response, however, can raise concerns about predestination and the very nature of free will. If God already knows our every choice, are our choices truly free? The question of whether divine foreknowledge is compatible with human freedom remains a significant theological challenge.

Furthermore, the problem of evil necessitates a reconsideration of the very nature of good and evil. Some theologians suggest that evil is not an independent force, but rather a privation of good, a deficiency or corruption of what is inherently good. This aligns with the concept of negative theology, which emphasizes the limits of human understanding in grasping the divine nature. Evil, from some perspective, is not a positive entity but a perversion or distortion of what ought to be. Darkness is not a thing, but an absence of light; and similarly, evil is not a substance but the absence or distortion of goodness.

This perspective, though elegant in its simplicity, struggles to address the tangible and destructive consequences of evil actions. The pain inflicted by a tyrant, the devastation wrought by a natural disaster, or the suffering endured by victims of injustice, are not simply the absence of good; they are real, profound, and deeply negative experiences. To dismiss these as mere privations minimizes the profound suffering the victims experience. While the conceptual distinction between a privation of good and a positive force of evil might hold some merit at a theoretical level, the reality of human suffering is a challenge that demands a more robust response.

Another way of addressing the problem of evil is through the lens of process theology. This theological perspective challenges the traditional concept of God as a completely immutable and transcendent being. Instead, it views God as participating actively in the world where He not only influences events but is also influenced by them.

In this model, God is not all-powerful in the sense of having absolute control over every event, but rather as having the power to influence who works to draw creation toward goodness. Evil, in this context, is not something that God is unable to prevent, but rather an unavoidable element of a dynamic and evolving cosmos. God's power is understood not as coercive control, but as persuasive influence that works within the constraints of a complex reality. This means that God is constantly working to mitigate suffering and to draw the world towards goodness, but this process is not always successful. Evil remains a challenge, a resistance to the divine influence. The focus shifts from a God who merely permits evil to a God who is actively engaged in overcoming it.

Finally, the problem of evil is inseparable from our understanding of human nature and the human condition. The very fact that we grapple with this question is a testament to our capacity for reason, empathy, and moral reflection. Our ability to recognize evil, to feel compassion, and to strive for justice, speaks to an inherent goodness within humanity. The presence of evil does not negate the possibility of good but rather highlights the tension and the inherent complexity of human existence. This complexity necessitates a nuanced response to the problem of evil and avoids simplistic answers. Meanwhile, it acknowledges the deep and persistent realities of suffering. Ultimately, grappling with the problem of evil is a process of spiritual and intellectual growth, which forces us to confront the limitations of our understanding, examine our beliefs with critical honesty, and strive for a deeper understanding of the nature of God and human condition. This ongoing struggle is not a sign of failure of faith, but rather a manifestation of its vital and enduring engagement with the fundamental questions of human existence. The quest for reconciliation between a benevolent God and a world of suffering remains an open and ongoing dialogue, which pushes the boundaries of theology, philosophy, and our understanding of ourselves. It is a continuous exploration that enriches our faith and compels us to remain engaged in compassionate action in the face of profound and persistent suffering.

The Manifestations of Evil: Understanding Different Forms of Harm

The exploration of evil necessitates a move to a concrete examination of its diverse manifestations, and not just abstract philosophical arguments. Evil is not a monolithic entity; rather, it presents itself in a multitude of forms, each demanding a nuanced

understanding. We can categorize these manifestations along various axes, as we recognize that these categories often overlap and interact in complex ways.

One fundamental distinction lies between individual and systemic evil. Individual evil encompasses acts of cruelty, violence, and malice, perpetrated by single individuals or small groups. These acts, which range from personal betrayal to mass murder, are driven by various psychological and emotional factors, among them greed, hatred, fear, and a desire for power. Understanding the motivation behind such acts is crucial to comprehending the nature of individual evil, although this understanding should never serve to excuse or minimize the suffering inflicted.

Examples of individual evil abound throughout history and contemporary society. The atrocities committed by individuals during times of war, the acts of terrorism driven by extremist ideologies, and the everyday occurrences of bullying, domestic violence, and hate crimes, all represent manifestations of individual evil. The depth and breadth of such acts are often shocking and disturbing and require serious reflection on the capacity for human cruelty. However, if we focus solely on individual acts of evil, we risk overlooking the larger, often more pervasive, structures that enable, and even encourage, such actions.

Systemic evil, in contrast, refers to the ways in which social structures, institutions, and systems perpetuate harm and injustice. It is not simply the result of the malicious intent of individuals, but rather the outcome from the interplay of various factors that include economic inequalities, political oppression, and cultural biases. Systemic evil can be far-reaching and deeply ingrained, and it can manifest in various forms of discrimination, exploitation, and oppression. It is often subtle and insidious and operates through seemingly neutral policies and practices that ultimately harm marginalized groups disproportionately.

Examples of systemic evil are widespread and deeply impactful. Historical ones include slavery and colonialism, and apartheid that systematically dehumanized and oppressed entire populations. Contemporary examples include systemic racism within law enforcement, healthcare disparities based on socioeconomic status, and the ongoing exploitation of workers in sweatshops and factories. These systems of oppression are rarely the product of a single malevolent actor, but rather the result of complex historical, economic, and social processes. Addressing systemic evil demands a multifaceted approach, which tackles the underlying structures and power dynamics that perpetuate injustice.

Another crucial distinction lies between intentional and unintentional evil. Intentional evil is characterized by a conscious desire to inflict harm or suffering. This is often associated with individual acts of cruelty or with systemic oppression driven by deliberate malice. However, unintentional evil encompasses actions or policies that inflict harm without a conscious intention to do so. This type of evil is often more difficult to identify and address, as it may be masked by good intentions or seemingly neutral motivations.

Examples of unintentional evil include environmental destruction caused by unsustainable practices, the unintended consequences of economic policies that exacerbate inequality, and the development of technologies that have unforeseen and devastating effects. The difficulty in identifying and addressing unintentional evil stems from the lack of explicit malicious intent. However, the harm caused is no less real, and recognizing the unintentional nature of evil should not diminish the responsibility to mitigate its effects.

A key aspect entails exploring and understanding the systemic and societal factors that make such unintentional harm possible. Are there mechanisms in place that prevent oversight and careful consideration of consequences? Are there inherent limitations in predicting all the ripple effects of actions, and how do we adjust accordingly?

The manifestation of evil can be understood through the lens of different religious and philosophical traditions. Many religions conceptualize evil as a force opposed to the Divine; a spiritual entity or principle that work actively against well. This perspective often places evil in direct conflict with God or other higher powers and creates a narrative of cosmic struggle. Other perspectives view evil as a product of human actions and choices; a distortion of human potential that results from free will.

It is crucial that we understand these varying interpretations, as we grapple with the complex nature of evil and its impact on human experience.

The impact of evil is multifaceted and profound and extends far beyond individual suffering. The consequences of evil acts and systems can have ripple effects throughout society, as they impact social cohesion, political stability, and economic development.

The lingering effects of historical atrocities, such as genocide or slavery, continue to manifest in contemporary social injustices. These effects highlight the pervasive and enduring nature of evil's influence, and the importance of actively addressing its various manifestations.

The psychological scars on individuals and communities can be profound and long-lasting, with the potential to extend to generations.

Trauma that results from evil acts can significantly impair mental and physical health, leaving individuals and communities struggling to cope with the aftermath of suffering. It, therefore, requires a multifaceted approach to address evil, an approach that combines individual and collective efforts. On an individual level, it is crucial to foster empathy, compassion, and moral responsibility. It is also imperative that we cultivate a strong moral compass and exercise critical thinking, as we identify and resist the allure of evil. Collective action, such as social movements that work toward addressing systemic injustice, and political reforms aimed at mitigating the causes of evil, are equally important. The path toward combating evil is a continuous journey, and requires continued engagement, critical reflection, and an unwavering commitment to justice and compassion. In this process, individuals should not only be able to recognize and resist evil, but also be actively involved in fostering good; that is, building structures that help people to flourish, promote social justice, and cultivate a culture of empathy and understanding. The goal is not merely to suppress or eliminate evil, but to build a world where goodness and compassion prevail. endeavor requires ongoing vigilance, commitment to justice, and constant effort that addresses the root causes of suffering; both individual and systemic. The nature of evil is complex and so must our approach to combat it.

Combating Evil Strategies for Promoting Good

Combating evil is not a passive endeavor; it is one that demands active engagement on multiple fronts. It requires a multifaceted strategy that addresses the immediate manifestations of evil as well as its underlying causes. While the previous section explored nature and various forms of evil, this section delves into the practical strategies that we can apply to confront it, as we promote good. These strategies encompass individual actions, collective efforts, and systemic change, all interwoven to create a more just and compassionate world.

One of the most fundamental strategies in combating evil is the cultivation of empathy and compassion. Empathy, the capacity to understand and share the feelings of another, is crucial in recognizing the suffering inflicted by evil. It allows us to connect with the victims of injustice and motivates us to act on their behalf. Compassion, in turn, compels us to alleviate suffering and promote the well-being of others. These qualities are not merely abstract virtues. They are essential tools in combating the dehumanizing effects of evil. By cultivating empathy and compassion, we create a moral framework that actively opposes the indifference and cruelty that often accompany evil acts. This cultivation begins with self-reflection, understanding our own biases and prejudices, and actively seeking out diverse perspectives. It involves engaging with narratives of suffering, fostering a deeper understanding of the experiences of others, and developing a heightened sensitivity to injustice. Furthermore, fostering empathy and compassion requires a commitment to listening actively and respectfully to the experiences of marginalized groups, and individuals who have been directly impacted by evil.

However, empathy and compassion alone are insufficient and must, therefore, be complemented by a commitment to justice. Justice, in this context, goes beyond simply punishing perpetrators of evil. It encompasses the pursuit of fairness and equity, as well as the restoration of harmony. It then becomes necessary to address the systemic causes of evil, reform unjust institutions, and ensure accountability for those who perpetrate harm. Justice requires a critical examination of power dynamics, as we recognize how imbalances in power contribute to the perpetuation of evil. It demands a commitment to dismantling oppressive structures and creating more equitable systems that foster human flourishing. This approach requires a willingness to confront uncomfortable truths, challenge established norms, and advocate for systemic change. Historical injustices serve as potent examples of the long-term effects of neglecting justice.

The legacies of slavery, colonialism, and apartheid continue to manifest in present-day social and economic inequalities and demonstrate the crucial need for ongoing efforts towards restorative justice and reconciliation.

In addition to empathy, compassion, and justice, it requires a strong moral compass and critical thinking skills to effectively combat evil. A strong moral compass enables us to identify and resist the allure of evil, both in its overt and subtle forms, while critical thinking equips us to objectively analyze situations, identify biases, and propaganda, and resist manipulation. It enables us to distinguish between genuine compassion and manipulation, ethical actions, and self-serving motives. This process involves engaging with diverse perspectives, challenging assumptions, and seeking out reliable information. It requires a commitment to evidence-based reasoning and a willingness to reconsider our beliefs as we consider new information. To develop these skills, one requires ongoing intellectual engagement, education, and a willingness to continuously question our assumptions. This is especially vital in combating the spread of misinformation and propaganda, which often serve as tools for justifying and perpetuating evil.

Collective action plays a pivotal role in combating evil. While individual actions are important, systemic change often requires collective effort. Social movements, advocacy groups, and community organizations play a crucial role in challenging oppressive systems, raising awareness about injustice, and mobilizing public support for reform. These efforts often involve long-term commitment, strategic planning, and sustained advocacy.

The history of social movements demonstrates the power of collective action in achieving significant social change, from the abolition of slavery to the advancement of civil rights. These movements highlight the importance of collaboration, organization, and persistence in combating evil and promoting justice.

Participation in such collective effort ranges from direct activism to support offered to organizations that work on the frontlines of social justice.

Furthermore, the prevention of evil requires proactive measures. It is, therefore, necessary to identify risk factors and vulnerabilities likely to lead to evil acts. To mitigate factors that contribute to violence, crime, and other forms of harm, it is important to invest in education, healthcare, and social support systems. Also, to create environments where evil is less likely to flourish, it is imperative that we strengthen community bonds, promote social cohesion, and foster inclusive societies. Early intervention programs that provide support and guidance can assist individuals at risk of engaging in harmful behavior, to make positive choices. This proactive approach represents a preventative strategy that can complement the reactive efforts made to address existing instances of evil.

The role of religious and philosophical traditions in combating evil is multifaceted. Many faiths offer ethical frameworks and moral guidance, which provide a foundation for ethical decision-making and commitment to justice. These traditions often emphasize compassion, forgiveness, and the importance of serving others.

However, we must acknowledge that religious beliefs have sometimes been misused to justify acts of violence and oppression. A critical approach to religious and philosophical teachings is essential if we are to discern their positive and negative contributions to the fight against evil. Critical engagement with these traditions, while acknowledging their potential for both good and harm, offers a pathway to understanding and combating the roots of evil.

Ultimately, the fight against evil is a continuous journey, not a destination. It requires ongoing vigilance, a commitment to justice, and a constant effort to address the root causes of suffering, both individual and systemic. It also demands a holistic approach that integrates individual actions, collective efforts, and systemic change. The goal is not merely to suppress or eliminate evil, but to build a world where goodness and compassion prevail; a world where justice is not merely a concept, but a lived reality for all. This requires a commitment to continue learning, adapt strategies, and remain steadfast in the pursuit of a more just and compassionate future. The complexities of evil demand a corresponding complexity in our approaches to combating it. The path forward necessitates a collaborative and persistent effort, which brings together individuals, communities, and institutions, in a shared commitment to building a better world. The challenges are immense, but the potential for positive transformation is equally profound.

The Power of Compassion: Overcoming Evil through Empathy

The capacity for empathy, the ability to step into another's shoe and genuinely feel their pain, is often overlooked as a potent weapon against evil. It is not merely a soft virtue but a strategic necessity in dismantling the structures that perpetuate malevolence. Empathy allows us to see humanity in those who perpetrate evil, understand the circumstances that may have contributed to their actions, while not condoning those actions. This understanding does not negate the harm caused, but it illuminates the complex web of factors that lead individuals down destructive paths. For instance, the child who grows up in a cycle of poverty and violence may be more likely to resort to crime as an adult. The reason is not that such a child is inherently evil, but because their environment has failed to provide them with alternatives. If we recognize this context, it does not mean we excuse criminal behavior; it only informs our strategies for intervention and rehabilitation, as we focus on addressing the root causes of the problem. We do not simply punish the symptoms.

Furthermore, empathy fosters a deep connection with the victims of evil. When we truly empathize with those suffering, we are more likely to be motivated to act on their behalf. The potent force of shared human experience erodes the indifference that allows evil to flourish. Consider the impact of personal narratives in highlighting the devastating consequences of hate crimes. A survivor's story, filled with raw emotion and detail, can have a far greater impact than a statistical report on the prevalence of hate crime. It humanizes the victims and shatters the anonymity that often shields perpetrators from accountability and public scrutiny. These narratives can transform casual observers into active participants in the fight against hatred and injustice. This personal connection transcends mere intellectual understanding; it fuels a visceral desire to create change, to ensure that others do not suffer the same fate.

Compassion, closely related to empathy, is an active response to suffering. It is the impulse to alleviate pain, help, and promote the well-being of those in need. While empathy provides understanding, compassion provides motivation for action. This active engagement is crucial in dismantling the structures that support evil.

Compassion demands that we recognize the suffering injustice causes, and also actively work to address it. This means challenging systems that perpetuate inequality, advocating for policies that support vulnerable populations, and contributing to initiatives that promote healing and reconciliation.

However, it is vital to distinguish between genuine compassion and manipulative sentimentality. Compassion is not simply feeling sorry for someone; it is a commitment to actively work to improve their situation. This requires a careful assessment of the situation, a critical analysis of power dynamics, and a willingness to challenge systems of oppression. It requires distinguishing between those who genuinely need help, and those who might exploit compassion for personal gain. It is a commitment to justice and equity, as we recognize that compassion without justice can be a form of paternalism, which can perpetuate the very inequalities it seeks to address.

The interplay between empathy, compassion, and justice is paramount. Empathy allows us to understand the root causes of evil, while compassion motivates us to act. Meanwhile, justice ensures that accountability is established, and harm is repaired. Justice, in this context, goes beyond retributive punishment; it encompasses restorative justice, focused on healing the wounds inflicted by evil and repairing the relationships damaged by injustice. The practices of restorative justice bring together victims, offenders, and community members to address the harm caused, and this allows for dialogue, accountability, and ultimately, reconciliation.

The power of forgiveness is also often overlooked in the fight against evil. Forgiveness does not equate to condoning the actions of the perpetrators of evil; rather, it releases the anger and resentment that can consume us at a personal level. It can be burdensome to hold onto anger and resentment, and it can prevent us from moving forward and focusing on building a more just and compassionate future. Forgiveness allows us to reclaim our own peace of mind and frees us from the destructive power of hatred. However, forgiveness should not be confused with reconciliation or impunity.

Accountability and reparations remain essential aspects of justice, even in the context of forgiveness. It is a nuanced approach that respects the needs of victims while offering a path towards healing, and reconciliation for all involved.

The pursuit of justice requires a critical examination of power dynamics. Evil often thrives in environments characterized by power imbalances, where certain groups hold disproportionate control over resources and opportunities. Addressing the root causes of evil necessitates dismantling these power structures and creating more equitable systems. This involves advocating for policies that promote social and economic justice, challenging discriminatory practices, and empowering marginalized groups. It requires a willingness to confront uncomfortable truths about our own complicity in systems of oppression, and a commitment to actively work towards systemic change.

Collective action is fundamental to combating evil. Individual acts of compassion and empathy are crucial, but systemic change necessitates collective efforts. Social movements, advocacy groups, and community organizations play a pivotal role in challenging oppressive systems. They raise awareness about injustice and mobilize public support for reform. These movements demonstrate the power of collaborative action in achieving significant societal changes. The civil rights movement, for example, exemplifies the transformative power of collective action in dismantling segregation and promoting racial equality. These historical precedents highlight the importance of sustained efforts, strategic planning, and a commitment to long-term goals.

In the fight against evil, it is vital to participate in these collective endeavors, whether through direct activism, or support for organizations that work on the frontlines of social justice, is vital.

Moreover, a proactive approach is necessary for prevention of evil, and. it involves identifying risk factors and vulnerabilities that can contribute to harmful behaviors. To mitigate the risk factors, it is important to invest in education, healthcare, and social support systems.

We can create environments where evil is less likely to flourish, by strengthening community bonds and fostering inclusive societies. Early intervention programs can help individuals at risk of engaging in harmful behavior, by providing them with support and guidance. This preventative approach complements the efforts made to address existing instances of evil and helps to create a comprehensive strategy for combating malevolence.

Religious and philosophical traditions offer valuable insight into the nature of evil and the strategies to mitigate it. Many faiths emphasize compassion, forgiveness, and the importance of serving others. However, critical engagement with these traditions is crucial. It is essential to acknowledge instances where religious beliefs have been misused to justify acts of violence and oppression.

A discerning approach allows us to identify the positive contributions of these traditions, while challenging their potential for misuse. This necessitates a commitment to interfaith dialogue, and a willingness to engage with diverse perspectives as we recognize the common ground in promoting peace and justice.

In conclusion, overcoming evil through empathy and compassion is not a passive endeavor; it is an ongoing process that requires constant vigilance and a commitment to systemic change. It demands a holistic approach that integrates individual actions, collective efforts, and systemic reforms. The aim is not merely to suppress evil, but to cultivate a world where compassion and justice prevail, where human flourishing is a lived reality for all. This requires continuous learning, adaptation, and a steadfast commitment to building a more just and compassionate future. It also requires acknowledgement of the profound challenges involved, while still being hopeful of the transformative power of human empathy and compassion. The path to a world free from the pervasive influence of evil is long and arduous, but it is worth walking, as it is illuminated by the enduring power of human compassion.

Existential Questions: Exploring the Meaning of Life

The preceding discussion emphasized the crucial role of empathy, compassion, and justice in combating evil. However, the fight against malevolence is inextricably linked to a deeper, more fundamental inquiry: the search for meaning in life itself. This pursuit, deeply personal and profoundly philosophical, underpins our motivations, our values, and ultimately, our actions. If life lacks inherent meaning, then the struggle against evil might appear arbitrary, a futile exercise in a meaningless universe. But if we can discover a purpose, a guiding principle beyond mere survival, then the fight against injustice takes on a new urgency and significance.

Existentialism, a philosophical movement that gained prominence in the 20th century, grapples directly with these questions. Thinkers like Albert Camus and Jean-Paul Sartre argued that existence precedes essence. This means we are born into the world without a pre-defined purpose, and it is through our choices and actions that we create our own meaning. This perspective can be both liberating and daunting. It liberates us from the constraints of predetermined roles and expectations and allows us to forge our own paths. Yet, it also throws us into a state of radical freedom, a freedom that can be overwhelming and even terrifying in its implications. The weight of responsibility in creating our own meaning can be heavy.

Camus, in his seminal work The Myth of Sisyphus, portrays Sisyphus, a mythical figure, as he explores the absurdity of human existence in a meaningless universe. Sisyphus is condemned to eternally roll a boulder up a hill, only to have it roll back down each time he nears the top. This Sisyphean task, Camus argues, reflects the human condition, which is a relentless struggle against insurmountable odds in a world devoid of inherent meaning. Yet, it is precisely in this absurdity that Camus finds a glimmer of hope. The rebellion against meaninglessness, reflected in Sisyphean's defiant act of continuing to strive despite the futility of the task, becomes the source of meaning itself. We find a kind of authenticity and purpose in the very act of resistance, the courageous embrace of the absurd.

Sartre, on the other hand, emphasized the concept of "bad faith," as reflected in the act of denying our freedom and responsibility. Individuals deny these when they conform to societal expectations or seek refuge in predetermined roles. He argued that we must embrace our radical freedom and acknowledge the full weight of our choices, as well as their consequences. This can be a challenging task, because it demands constant self-reflection and a willingness to confront the potential for failure. However, it is through this authentic engagement with our freedom that we create genuine meaning in our lives. The search for meaning, according to Sartre, is not a passive pursuit, but an active creation that is a constant process of self-definition and self-transcendence.

In contrast to the existentialist perspective, many religious and spiritual traditions offer a pre-defined sense of purpose. These traditions often posit a divine creator, and a cosmic plan that provides a framework for understanding our place in the universe and our reasons for being. The meaning of life, in these frameworks, is often tied to fulfilling God's will, serving humanity, or achieving spiritual enlightenment. However, the very diversity of religious beliefs demonstrates the challenge faced by trying to arrive at a universally accepted answer. Different religions and spiritual paths offer dramatically different visions of purpose, and this leads to potential conflict and disagreement.

Furthermore, even within a single religious tradition, the interpretation of sacred texts and doctrines can vary widely. The varying understandings of meaning and purpose range from a focus on individual salvation, to a commitment to social justice and collective liberation. The challenges of reconciling faith with reason, science, and ethical dilemmas also raise complex questions about the nature of truth and the validity of religious claims. The search for meaning within religious frameworks frequently necessitates a critical and nuanced approach, which engages with the complexities of faith and doubt, as well as tradition and innovation.

Beyond religion, humanist philosophies offer another avenue through which to find meaning. Humanism emphasizes the value and dignity of human life, and focuses on reason, ethics, and social justice. Humanists find meaning in human relationships, creative endeavors, intellectual pursuits, and contributions to society. They believe that we can create a meaningful existence through our interactions with others and through our efforts to improve the world around us. This approach places emphasis on human agency and responsibility and hence aligns with the existentialist focus on self-creation. However, humanism also recognizes the importance of community and cooperation, which suggests that individual meaning is deeply interconnected with collective well-being.

The pursuit of meaning is not limited to grand philosophical systems or religious doctrines. It is also reflected in our everyday experiences, our relationships, work, and hobbies. We find meaning when we discover our passions, develop our talents, connect with others, contribute to a cause we believe in, and experience moments of joy, wonder, and gratitude. These everyday experiences often provide a sense of purpose and fulfillment that is deeply personal and profoundly meaningful. The meaning of life, therefore, is not a singular, universally applicable concept, but a deeply personal and evolving understanding. Our individual experiences, values, and beliefs help to shape this understanding.

In the context of fighting evil, the search for meaning becomes particularly crucial. If our lives are inherently meaningful, or we believe in a larger purpose beyond our individual existence, then the struggle against injustice takes on new significance. The fight against evil becomes not merely a response to immediate harm, but an affirmation of our values. It also depends on our beliefs and contributes to greater good. Whether our meaning is derived from existentialist principles, religious faith, humanist values, or a combination of these and other sources, the conviction that life has meaning can be a powerful motivating force in the pursuit of justice and compassion. Without a sense of purpose, the fight against evil may seem daunting, or even hopeless. But with a clear understanding of our own values and their connection to a larger meaning, we find the strength and resolve to persevere. The journey to uncover the meaning of life is a continuous exploration, deeply personal, and endlessly fascinating, and in the heart of this journey lies the motivation to fight for a better world. That world is imbued with justice, compassion, and an unwavering belief in the inherent worth of every human life. The struggle against evil is, in essence, a manifestation of our profound aspirations, and a testament to our belief in goodness that can flourish even in the darkest of times. It reflects the deep-seated yearning for meaning, a yearning that binds us together in our shared quest for a more compassionate and just future.

The Pursuit of Meaning: Identifying Personal Values and Goals

The preceding exploration of existentialism, religious belief, and humanism offers a diverse landscape of perspectives on meaning, yet the question remains: How do we personally translate these philosophical and theological frameworks into a lived experience of purpose? The search for meaning is not a passive intellectual exercise. It is an active process of self-discovery, a journey of inward exploration that leads to a clearer understanding of our values and aspirations. This understanding forms the bedrock upon which we build a meaningful life, one that resonates deeply with our individual selves and allows us to engage fully with the world around us.

The first step in this process involves a rigorous examination of our own values. What principles guide our decisions? What qualities do we admire most in ourselves and others? Are we driven by a desire for power, wealth, or recognition? Or are we motivated by compassion, justice, creativity, or knowledge? It is not easy to answer these questions. Moreover, the process of self-reflection can be challenging and sometimes uncomfortable. We may discover inconsistencies between our stated values and our actual actions, and this reveals areas where we need to align our behavior with our ideals.

Consider the following examples: Someone who claims to value honesty might find themselves tempted to bend the truth to avoid an unpleasant consequence. A person who professes a commitment to environmental sustainability might find themselves indulging in environmentally damaging habits. These discrepancies are not necessarily signs of moral failure, but rather opportunities for growth and self-improvement. Recognizing these inconsistencies is the first step towards aligning our actions with our values, which fosters a greater sense of integrity and authenticity.

Journaling can be a powerful tool in this process of self-discovery. If we write about our thoughts, feelings, and experiences regularly, it can help us identify patterns and themes that are recurrent in our lives. This illuminates our underlying values and motivations. Prompts such as "What makes me feel truly alive?" or "What are my deepest regrets?" can be particularly helpful in uncovering our core values. They can also help identify areas where we might be straying from our path. The act of writing itself facilitates introspection and allows us to delve deeper into our subconscious. This helps to unearth the guiding principles that shape our lives.

Beyond introspection, we can engage in meaningful conversations with trusted friends, family members, mentors, or therapists, in order to benefit from valuable external perspectives. We can also talk about our values and aspirations with others to articulate them more clearly, and to receive feedback that challenges our assumptions and expands our understanding of ourselves. These conversations can be transformative, in a manner to help us see ourselves in a new light. They can also help us gain a deeper understanding of our own strengths and weaknesses.

Once we have a clearer understanding of our personal values, the next step is to define our goals. What do we want to achieve in life? What legacy do we want to leave behind? These are profound questions that require careful consideration. Our goals should be aligned with our values, which would ensure that our actions are congruent with our deepest beliefs. It is crucial to set realistic and achievable goals as it avoids the pitfalls where we set ourselves up for disappointment. We run the risk of being overly ambitious as we set our goals, setting unattainable goals.

Goal setting is not merely a matter of identifying what we want. It also requires planning and strategizing. When we break down large goals, particularly the overarching goals, into smaller, more manageable steps, it makes them less daunting and more achievable. The process involves identifying the resources we need, the likely obstacles, and the steps we need to take to overcome those obstacles. It is a continuous process of adjustment and refinement, a dynamic interplay between planning and adapting to changing circumstances.

Consider the example of someone who values creativity and wants to write a novel. This overarching goal can be broken down into smaller, more manageable steps: developing a compelling plot, creating believable characters, writing a daily word count, seeking feedback from beta readers, and revising the manuscript. Each of these steps contribute to the larger goal, which makes the entire process less overwhelming and more rewarding.

The pursuit of meaning extends beyond personal goals to incorporate contributions to something larger than ourselves. Such contributions could be in the form of volunteer services to a charitable organization, advocacy for social justice, engagement in artistic expression, or contribution to scientific discovery. These activities connect us with a larger purpose and provide a sense of fulfillment and belonging that transcends our individual aspirations. They often provide a sense of shared purpose and community, thus connecting us to others who share our values and passions.

This sense of contributing to something larger is essential to preventing a sense of isolation and meaninglessness. As we engage with the wider community, both local and global, we see our own struggles and aspirations reflected in the lives of others. We find common ground, shared values, and mutual support that strengthens our own individual pursuit for meaning. This participation also fosters a sense of responsibility towards our community and fosters a sense of active citizenship and a commitment to improving the world around us.

The pursuit of meaning is a continuous journey, not a destination. Our values and goals may evolve over time as we grow and learn, as our experiences shape our perspectives, and as our understanding of ourselves deepens. This ongoing process of self-reflection and adjustment is essential for maintaining a sense of purpose and fulfillment throughout our lives. The path to meaning is not a straight line Rather, it is a winding road with unexpected twists and turns. Therefore, it requires patience, persistence, and a willingness to adapt.

It is crucial to remember that setbacks and failures are inevitable aspects of this journey. The challenges, though difficult, offer valuable opportunities for learning and growth. They help us refine our understanding of ourselves, our values, and our goals. If we embrace these challenges and learn from our mistakes, we can emerge stronger and more resilient and better equipped to navigate the complexities of life as we pursue our meaning with renewed vigor. The true measure of our success is not the absence of setbacks, but our capacity to learn from them and continue our path toward living a life of meaningful and fulfilment. The pursuit of meaning is a lifelong endeavor, a constant process of self-discovery and refinement. It is also on this ongoing journey that we discover the true depth and richness of our own humanity.

Finding Fulfillment: Aligning Actions with Values

The preceding discussion highlighted the crucial role of self reflection in identifying our core values. However, understanding our values is only half the battle. True fulfillment stems from actively aligning our actions with these deeply held principles. This is not a passive process but one that requires conscious effort, consistent self-monitoring, and a willingness to adapt our behavior to reflect our ideals. The discrepancy between our stated values and our actual actions creates internal conflict, and this leads to feelings of dissonance and a sense of unfulfillment. This is the case even when these discrepancies are seemingly minor. This internal conflict is a powerful indicator that there is need for recalibration.

One of the most effective methods for aligning actions with values is mindful decision-making. Whenever you need to make any significant decision, whether it be accepting a new job, making a significant purchase, or engaging in a particular social interaction, pause and consider how this action aligns with your core values. Does the decision you want to make reflect honesty, integrity, compassion, or any other value you hold dear? If the answer is no, or even if you are hesitant, it is crucial that you explore the reasons behind that hesitation. This conscious examination can reveal underlying conflicts, and help you make choices that are more congruent with your values. The process itself is a form of self-education that allows you to better understand your own motivations and guiding principles.

Consider the example of someone who values environmental sustainability but frequently drives a gas-guzzling vehicle.

If they recognize this inconsistency, they might decide to explore alternative transportation methods, such as cycling, public transport, or a more fuel-efficient car. This action is driven by a desire to align their behavior with their values, and it leads to a greater sense of integrity and a more authentic expression of their commitment to the environment. The shift is not necessarily about drastic, immediate changes, but rather a commitment to gradual, mindful adjustments that bring actions in line with ideals.

Similarly, someone who values strong family relationships might discover they have been neglecting their family due to an overcommitment to their career. Once they recognize this value-action discrepancy, they could reassess their priorities and set boundaries at work and ultimately dedicate more time and attention to the family. This intentional realignment, where one aligns actions with deeply held values, improves family relationships and fosters a deeper sense of purpose and fulfillment.

This process requires self-compassion. We are all human and it is inevitable that at times we shall fall short of our ideals. Instead of succumbing to self-criticism and discouragement, we need to acknowledge the shortcomings as opportunities for growth and learning. Every instance of misalignment offers a chance for self-reflection, a chance to understand the reason for acting in a way that contradicts our values. It is also an opportunity to implement strategies that avoid similar inconsistencies in the future. This self-compassion fosters a virtuous cycle of growth and refinement, which enhances the journey of aligning actions with values.

Furthermore, in this process, it is crucial that one sets realistic and achievable goals. Attempting to overhaul one's entire life overnight to perfectly align with their values is a recipe for burnout and failure. Instead, the focus should be on making small, incremental changes. Start with one area where you feel the discrepancy is most prominent, and work on aligning your actions there. Once you have achieved success in that area, move on to another. This gradual approach fosters a sense of accomplishment and encourages continued progress. Meanwhile, it helps to build momentum towards greater alignment.

The use of external accountability can also greatly aid this process.

Sharing your values and goals with trusted friends, family, or a mentor can provide valuable support and encouragement. These individuals can offer perspectives you might not have considered, hold you accountable to your commitments, and celebrate your successes along the way. The support network enhances the possibility of sustained commitment and bolsters your resolve and motivation in times of challenge. This external accountability can transform a private journey into a shared experience and foster deeper connections while amplifying the sense of purpose and accomplishment.

Regular journaling also plays a vital role. When you document your progress, reflect on your successes and challenges, and analyze your motivations, you can understand your personal growth deeper. Likewise, when you track your efforts, you can identify patterns in your behavior and gain insight into the areas you consistently fall short. This ongoing process of self-assessment is fundamental for maintaining momentum, fostering continuous self-improvement, and reinforcing the alignment between actions and values.

Beyond personal introspection and external accountability, it is equally critical to actively seek opportunities that align with your values. This might involve volunteering for a cause you deeply care about, joining a community group that shares your interests, or pursuing educational or professional opportunities that reflect your values. By consciously integrating your values into various aspects of your life, you create a more cohesive and fulfilling existence. This active pursuit of value-aligned experiences deepens your sense of purpose and strengthens your commitment to living authentically.

The alignment of actions with values should not be a one-time achievement, buts a continuous process that requires ongoing effort and self-reflection. Life is dynamic, which means circumstances change and our understanding of ourselves and our values evolve over time. Therefore, regular reevaluation and adjustment are necessary if we are to maintain congruence between our actions and our deepest convictions. Embracing the inherent fluidity of this process fosters a sense of openness and adaptability, which allows for personal growth and greater life satisfaction. It is through this continuous process of self-discovery and refinement that we ultimately find true fulfillment and a deep sense of meaning in our lives. The journey itself, with its inherent challenges and triumphs, becomes a testament that we are committed to living a life of purpose and integrity.

This consistent self-assessment and refinement is what allows for authentic personal growth and deepens the sense of meaning and fulfillment.

Overcoming Nihilism: Finding Hope in a Meaningless World

The preceding exploration where we align actions with values provides a crucial foundation for confronting nihilism- the belief that life is inherently without meaning, purpose, or intrinsic value. While the previous section focused on the individual's internal compass, nihilism challenges the very existence of that compass and suggest that any meaning we ascribe to life is merely a self-constructed illusion. This perspective can be profoundly unsettling, and can lead to feelings of despair, apathy, and a sense of profound emptiness. However, even within the framework of a seemingly meaningless universe, hope and purpose can be found. However, you cannot expect to find these by denying nihilism, but by understanding and engaging with its implications.

One approach to overcoming nihilism involves recognizing the limitations of seeking inherent, pre-ordained meaning. Instead of searching for a cosmic blueprint or divine mandate, we can cultivate meaning by creating personal values and goals. This is not tantamount to denying the possibility of a meaningless universe, but rather a shift in perspective that puts focus on what we can control —our actions, choices, and the relationships we forge. The absence of inherent meaning does not necessitate a life devoid of purpose Instead; it opens the door to a radical freedom that allows us to create our own meaning.

This creative freedom allows for a profound sense of autonomy and self-determination. We are not puppets bound by pre-determined scripts, but authors of our own narratives. This realization, though initially daunting, can be incredibly liberating. It allows us to define our own values, pursue our own goals, and establish our own standards for success. There is a sense of agency, even within a potentially meaningless universe, and it can be a powerful antidote to the despair often associated with nihilistic thinking.

However, the creation of meaning requires active engagement.

Passive acceptance of a meaningless universe only reinforces feelings of apathy and despair, yet meaning can be cultivated through action, pursuing projects, fostering relationships, and contributing to something larger than oneself. This active creation of meaning might involve artistic expression, scientific discovery, social activism, or dedicated service to others. The key lies in identifying activities that resonate with our deepest values, then pursuing them with passion and commitment.

Consider the work of Albert Camus, who's philosophical explorations of absurdism offered a powerful alternative to nihilistic despair. Absurdism is the conflict between the human desire for meaning and the meaningless universe, and Camus did not deny the inherent absurdity of existence. Nevertheless, he argued that human response should be one of passionate rebellion, which means embracing life despite its apparent meaninglessness. This rebellion is not about fighting against the universe but about embracing life's inherent uncertainties while finding joy and purpose in the face of them. His philosophy emphasized the importance of living authentically, embracing the present moment, and finding meaning in the act of living itself. This should happen regardless of any external validation or pre-ordained purpose.

Similarly, the existentialist philosophers like Jean-Paul Sartre and Simone de Beauvoir emphasized the freedom and responsibility inherent in the human condition. They argued that humans are condemned to be free. This means we are not pre-programmed or determined by external forces. However, this freedom comes with the responsibility of creating our own meaning and values.

Therefore, existentialism, offers a framework within which to confront nihilism, which is by putting emphasis on the importance of individual choice and action in creating a meaningful life. It is a philosophy of empowerment that encourages us to take ownership of our lives; also, to create our own narratives even in the face of existential uncertainty.

Another crucial aspect of overcoming nihilism lies in cultivating strong relationships and connections with others. The human experience is inherently social, and meaningful relationships can provide a sense of belonging, purpose, and emotional support. Sharing our lives with others, contributing to their well-being, and experiencing the reciprocal love and support that comes from close relationships, can counter the isolating experience of nihilistic despair. These relationships provide a context for making meaning and offer a sense of community and shared purpose.

Furthermore, the pursuit of knowledge and understanding can also serve as a powerful antidote to nihilism. We can broaden our perspectives, deepen our understanding of the human condition, and connect to something larger than ourselves by engaging in art, literature, philosophy, science, and other forms of intellectual exploration. Learning about different cultures, historical periods, and scientific discoveries can expand our sense of what is possible and help us appreciate the complexity and wonder of the world around us. This pursuit of knowledge, far from being a distraction from the existential angst of nihilism, can enrich our lives and provide a framework within which to find purpose and meaning.

The practice of mindfulness and meditation can also play a significant role in coping with nihilistic feelings. These practices encourage us to focus on the present moment, to appreciate the sensory experiences of our lives, and to cultivate a sense of acceptance and peace. By grounding ourselves in the present, we can find a sense of stability and resilience in the face of existential uncertainty. Mindfulness is not about denying or escaping the

challenges of life but rather engaging with them with greater awareness and equanimity.

Finally, it's crucial to recognize the importance of self-compassion in navigating feelings of meaninglessness. Nihilism can be a deeply unsettling perspective, and it is natural to experience feelings of fear, anxiety, and despair. Instead of judging or criticizing ourselves for these feelings, we should approach them with self-compassion as we recognize that they are normal human responses to challenging philosophical questions. Self-compassion allows us to engage with our feelings without being overwhelmed by them. It also allows us to create space for reflection and growth.

In conclusion, overcoming nihilism is not about denying the potential meaninglessness of the universe. Rather, it is about finding meaning and purpose within the context of that meaninglessness.

It is a process of actively creating our own values, pursuing our goals, fostering meaningful relationships, and cultivating a sense of self-compassion. It is a journey of self-discovery and creation, where we are the authors of our own lives even in a universe that may appear devoid of inherent purpose. This creative engagement, this active rebellion against the void, is precisely what allows us to find hope and purpose, even in a seemingly meaningless world. The freedom inherent in nihilism, paradoxically, becomes the very source of our ability to define and create meaning for ourselves. It is through this active engagement with life that we discover our own unique purpose despite its inherent uncertainties, and a deep and profound appreciation for the preciousness of existence. The journey to confront nihilism is not one of despair, but one of empowering self-discovery and authentic self-creation.

Creating a Meaningful Life Strategies for Purposeful Living

Building upon the framework established in our discussion of nihilism and its implications, we now turn to the practical application of creating a meaningful life. The previous section laid the groundwork by demonstrating that the absence of inherent, pre-ordained meaning does not equate to a life devoid of purpose.

Instead, it presents an opportunity—a radical freedom—to define and construct our own individual narratives of meaning. This section delves into the concrete strategies that can facilitate this process of self-creation and purposeful living.

The first, and perhaps most fundamental, step in building a meaningful life is the establishment of clear, personal goals. These goals should not be imposed upon us by societal pressures or external expectations. Instead, they should stem from a deep understanding of our own values and aspirations.

It requires introspection and honest self-reflection to identify these core values. What truly matters to us? What principles guide our decisions and shape our interactions with the world? Are we driven by a desire for creative expression, intellectual exploration, social justice, or perhaps a commitment to personal growth and well-being? Answering these questions helps us define the compass that will guide our journey toward a purposeful life.

Once we identify our core values, we can begin to formulate goals that align with them. These goals should be specific, measurable, achievable, relevant, and time-bound (SMART), which offers a concrete path toward realizing our aspirations. For example, if our core value is contributing to social justice, a SMART goal might be: "To volunteer at a local homeless shelter for two hours every Saturday for the next six months." Similarly, if our core value is personal growth, a SMART goal might be: "To complete a course in mindfulness meditation within the next three months." The specificity and measurability of these goals ensure that our efforts are focused, and that we can track our progress toward meaningful accomplishment.

Furthermore, our goals should not be limited to grand, overarching ambitions. Meaning can also be found in the smaller, everyday actions that align with our values. The consistent practice of small acts of kindness, generosity, or self-care can contribute significantly to a sense of purpose and well-being. These acts might be as simple as offering a listening ear to a friend, performing a random act of kindness, or engaging in regular exercise. The cumulative effect of these seemingly small acts can be surprisingly powerful in shaping our overall sense of meaning and fulfillment. It is in the consistency of these smaller actions that a deep and lasting sense of purpose can take root.

In addition to setting goals, it is essential to cultivate our passions in order to create a meaningful life. Passions are those activities that ignite our enthusiasm, stimulate our creativity, and bring us a sense of joy and fulfillment. They are not merely hobbies or distractions, but rather sources of deep personal engagement and self-expression.

To identify and pursue our passions, we need to explore our interests, experiment with different activities, and discover what truly resonates with us on a deep level. This exploration might involve taking classes, joining clubs, engaging in creative projects, or simply spending time reflecting on what truly energizes us. The discovery of our passions can be a transformative process, which can lead to a renewed sense of purpose and direction.

The pursuit of passions also connects directly to the concept of flow, a state of intense focus and engagement where time seems to disappear and we feel completely absorbed in our activity. This state of flow, often associated with peak experiences of creativity and productivity, is a potent source of meaning and satisfaction. When we are in the flow, we are not merely performing a task rather, we are fully present and engaged in the process, as we find intrinsic reward in the activity itself. It is vital to cultivate conditions that allow for regular experiences of flow, to foster a meaningful and fulfilling life.

Another crucial element in creating a meaningful life involves contributing to something larger than oneself. To accomplish this, we need to connect our individual actions to a wider purpose, whether through volunteer work, social activism, creative endeavors beneficial to the community, or simply acts of kindness and generosity.

This contribution can provide a profound sense of purpose and meaning. It can also remind us that our lives are interconnected, and that our actions have the potential to positively impact the world around us. It is in this interconnectedness that we find a deeper understanding of our place within the grander scheme of things, and we move beyond a solely individualistic perspective to one that embraces shared humanity.

This sense of contribution can take many forms, among them advocating for social justice, environmental protection, or artistic expression that resonates with other people. Other possible forms include mentoring others, fostering strong relationships, or simply offering support to those in need. The key is to identify areas where we can make a genuine difference, align our actions with our values, and contribute to a cause or community that resonates with our sense of purpose. The act of giving back, which is part of contributing to something greater than ourselves, is profoundly fulfilling. It enriches both the lives of those we serve and our own sense of meaning.

Furthermore, to lead a meaningful life, it is vital to cultivate strong relationships and foster a sense of belonging. Human beings are inherently social creatures, which means our well-being is intrinsically linked to our connections with other people. Meaningful relationships provide emotional support, a sense of belonging, and a shared context within which life's experiences make sense. Investing time and effort in building and nurturing relationships is a crucial investment in our overall well-being and sense of purpose. These relationships offer mutual support, understanding, and a shared experience of life's joys and challenges. It is within these intimate and supportive connections that a resilient and meaningful life can truly flourish.

Finally, embracing lifelong learning and a commitment to personal growth plays a critical role in creating a meaningful life. This means we need to actively seek new knowledge, develop new skills, and continually challenge ourselves to expand our horizons. This pursuit of learning can take many forms, from formal education to self-directed study; or from creative endeavors to engaging with different cultures and perspectives. The process of learning itself is inherently enriching, and it fosters intellectual stimulation, personal growth, and a sense of accomplishment. By embracing a mindset of continuous learning, we remain open to new experiences, challenges, and opportunities for growth and development.

In conclusion, creating a meaningful life is not a passive endeavor but rather an active, ongoing process of self-discovery, goal setting, and contribution. It requires introspection, self-awareness, and a commitment to aligning our actions with our values and passions.

By setting clear goals, cultivating our passions, contributing to something larger than ourselves, nurturing strong relationships, and embracing lifelong learning, we can create a life filled with purpose, meaning, and enduring fulfillment, even within the context of a seemingly meaningless universe. The journey is one of continuous creation and self-discovery, a testament to the resilience and creative capacity of the human spirit. The absence of inherent meaning is not condemnation, but an invitation to become the authors of our own lives; also, to craft narratives filled with purpose and lasting significance.

Synthesizing Key Concepts: A Holistic Perspective

Having explored the diverse landscapes of human experience, and our attempts to grapple with the Divine, we now arrive at a synthesis of these interwoven threads. This concluding section does not offer definitive answers. The ongoing dialogue about humanity and Divine remains, but it is, by its very nature, open-ended.

It aims to provide a holistic framework, a lens through which to view the myriad perspectives the book presents. We have examined the historical evolution of religious beliefs, from ancient animistic practices to the sophisticated theologies of modern faiths. We have also delved into the philosophical debates that surround the existence of God, the problem of evil, and the nature of faith itself. We have explored the psychological and sociological dimensions of religion and recognized its profound influence on individual lives and societal structures. Now, we seek to integrate these insights as we acknowledge the complexities and contradictions inherent in the human search for the Divine.

The journey has been, in many ways, a testament to the inherent human need for meaning and purpose. Through cultures and throughout history, humans have consistently sought explanations regarding the universe and their place within it. This quest has not always been expressed through formal religious frameworks; sometimes it has been done through myths, art, philosophy, or simply in the quiet contemplation of nature. The forms may vary, but the underlying impulse, which is the desire to understand, to connect, and to find meaning remains a constant. This deep-seated yearning is, arguably, the bedrock upon which the ongoing dialogue between humanity and the Divine is built.

One of the most significant themes that emerges from our exploration is the inherent tension between faith and reason. Throughout history, these two forces have often been presented as diametrically opposed, locked in an eternal struggle for dominance. Yet, a closer examination reveals a more nuanced relationship. Reason, with its emphasis on logic and empirical evidence, offers a critical framework within which to evaluate claims and explore the world around us. Faith, on the other hand, often transcends the limitations of reason, embracing belief and trust even in the absence of definitive proof. The tension does not arise necessarily from their incompatibility, but from their different approaches to understanding reality. A truly holistic perspective recognizes the validity and limitations of both faith and reason and encourages a dialogue rather than a conflict.

The most fruitful approaches to understanding the relationship between humanity and the Divine often involve a synthesis of these seemingly opposing forces. A reasoned faith, for example, critically examines its own beliefs, while maintaining a commitment to its core tenets.

Furthermore, the concept of experience plays a crucial role in shaping our understanding of the Divine. While theological doctrines and philosophical arguments offer valuable frameworks for understanding religious beliefs, personal experiences often hold a disproportionate influence on individual faith. Mystical experiences, moments of profound connection, and encounters with suffering can fundamentally alter an individual's perception of the Divine. These subjective experiences, while difficult to quantify or objectively verify, are nonetheless powerful shapes of belief and spiritual understanding. A holistic perspective acknowledges the importance of these lived experiences and recognizes their profound impact on individual faith and the collective religious landscape.

Moreover, the impact of social and cultural factors on religious belief cannot be overstated. Religion is not a static entity that exists in isolation. On the contrary, it is surrounded by social and cultural contexts within which it operates. Religion is a dynamic force, shaped and reshaped by the societies in which it flourishes. Social structures, cultural norms, and historical events all play a significant role in determining the forms that religious beliefs take. A critical examination of religion necessitates an understanding of its socio-cultural embeddedness, and recognition that the expressions of faith are often products of their specific historical and social environments.

Our exploration also highlighted the diverse range of religious experiences and expressions across cultures and throughout history.

From the polytheistic pantheons of ancient civilizations to the monotheistic traditions of the Abrahamic faiths, the variety of religious beliefs and practices is astounding. This diversity, rather than signify a lack of coherence, speaks to the inherent human capacity for creativity and adaptation; also, to the search for meaning in the face of life's uncertainties. Recognizing this diversity is essential for fostering interfaith dialogue and understanding, moving beyond simplistic generalizations to embrace the richness and complexity of religious experience. The multiplicity of religious expressions should be seen not as a threat to a unified understanding of the Divine, but rather as an indication of the many paths that humans have taken in their quest to connect with something greater than themselves.

The ongoing dialogue between humanity and Divine is not a debate with a predetermined outcome. It is an evolving conversation, a process of continuous questioning, exploration, and re-evaluation. New discoveries in science, advancements in philosophy, shifts in social and cultural contexts, all contribute to the ongoing conversation, and they enrich our understanding of both humanity and the Divine. It is a conversation that requires openness, humility, and a willingness to engage with diverse perspectives, as they challenge our preconceived notions and embrace the complexities of faith, reason, and experience. The pursuit of truth in this context is not about achieving a final, definitive answer, but engaging in a lifelong process of learning, growth, and mutual understanding. The journey itself, which entails the continuous striving to understand our place in the universe, and our relationship with the Divine, is perhaps more significant than arriving at any single conclusion.

Furthermore, the historical narrative of this ongoing dialogue reveals a constant interplay between the established religious institutions and individual experiences. While organized religions offer established doctrines, rituals, and communities, individual experiences of faith often challenge, reinterpret, and even transcend these established structures. The tension between institutionalized religion and individual spirituality is an ongoing dynamic, which shapes the evolution of religious beliefs and practices. A healthy religious landscape acknowledges this tension and fosters space for both communal worship and personal spiritual exploration. The individual's search for meaning is not necessarily in opposition to institutional structures, and it can contribute to the evolution and vitality of the faith itself. The continuous exchange between individual spirituality and religious institutions is essential for a vibrant and meaningful religious life.

Finally, this concluding section is not meant to serve as a definitive statement, but as a springboard for continued reflection. The relationship between humanity and the Divine is a complex and deeply personal matter, resistant to simple explanations or conclusive answers. The insights and perspectives explored in this book are intended to stimulate further thought and dialogue, and to prompt readers to engage in their own individual explorations of faith, reason, and the search for meaning. The ongoing conversation is, ultimately, one that everyone must engage in personally, and draw upon their own experiences, beliefs, and understandings. The journey towards understanding is a personal one, fueled by curiosity, humility, and the enduring human desire to connect with something greater than oneself. This is a journey of lifelong learning, where we are constantly evolving and reshaping our understanding of the world and our place within it. The dialogue continues.

The Continuing Journey: Embracing Ongoing Spiritual Growth

The conclusion of our exploration into the dialogue between humanity and the Divine is a beginning and not an ending. Here, we recognize that the search for meaning, which constitutes the yearning for connection with something transcendent, is a lifelong journey, a continuous process of growth and transformation. This ongoing spiritual growth is not a linear progression towards some ultimate destination, but a cyclical process of questioning, learning, and re-evaluation. It is a process constantly shaped by our evolving understanding of ourselves and the world around us.

One of the key aspects of this continuing journey lies in the cultivation of self-awareness. Genuine spiritual growth requires a willingness to honestly examine our own beliefs, biases, and assumptions. This involves critical self-reflection, a conscious effort to understand the sources and influences that shape our perspectives on the Divine. Are our beliefs based on reasoned conviction, inherited traditions, personal experiences, or a combination of these factors? Understanding the origins of our beliefs is crucial if we are to discern their validity; also, for identifying areas where further exploration or revision may be necessary. This process necessitates intellectual honesty, and a willingness to confront discomforting truths even if it challenges our deeply held convictions. The journey of spiritual growth often involves letting go of outdated or inaccurate beliefs, while making space for new insights and perspectives.

Furthermore, continuous learning is essential for maintaining a vibrant and evolving spiritual life. This involves engaging with a diverse range of sources, including theological texts, philosophical treatises, scientific discoveries and the wisdom of different cultures and traditions. We must cultivate a receptivity to new ideas and perspectives, even those that challenge our existing beliefs. This open-mindedness is crucial for broadening our understanding of the complex relationship between humanity and the Divine and moving beyond limited or parochial perspectives. The pursuit of knowledge in this context is not simply intellectual exercise; it is a spiritual practice that enriches our capacity for empathy, understanding, and compassion. It allows us to appreciate the multifaceted nature of the human experience and the diverse ways in which people have engaged with the Divine throughout history.

The integration of reason and faith is another crucial aspect of continued spiritual growth. As we have previously discussed, these two forces are not necessarily opposed, but rather complementary approaches to understanding reality. Reason provides a framework for critical inquiry and allows us to evaluate claims and assess the evidence supporting our beliefs. Faith, on the other hand, embraces trust and belief, often extending beyond the realm of empirical verification.

The integration of these two aspects requires a delicate balance, a nuanced approach that values both logical rigor and subjective experience of faith. A truly robust spiritual life incorporates both intellectual inquiry and personal experience and creates a holistic framework for understanding the Divine. This integration is not a simple compromise but a dynamic interplay, a constant negotiation between faith and reason that constantly refine and shape our understanding.

Experiential learning plays a significant role in this ongoing process. While theological doctrines and philosophical arguments offer valuable frameworks, personal experiences shape our spiritual lives profoundly. Moments of profound connection, encounters with suffering, acts of compassion, and encounters with nature can profoundly alter our perspectives on the Divine. These subjective experiences, though difficult to articulate or objectively verify, are powerful catalysts for spiritual growth. They challenge our preconceived notions, push the boundaries of our understanding, and often lead to transformative insights. Keeping a journal, practicing mindfulness, or engaging in contemplative practices, can help us to process and integrate these experiences, and deepen our understanding of our own spiritual journey. For a truly authentic and meaningful spiritual life, it is crucial to recognize and value the importance of these lived experiences.

Furthermore, the social and cultural contexts in which we live profoundly shape our spiritual understanding. Religion is not an isolated entity, but a dynamic force embedded within social structures, cultural norms, and historical events. It is crucial to understand these contextual influences for the sake of interpreting religious beliefs and practices accurately. For example, the historical evolution of a particular religious tradition, its interaction with other cultures, and the social conditions under which it has flourished, all influence its present-day expression.

If we are to genuinely appreciate religious diversity, we need to understand these contextual factors and move beyond simplistic comparisons and judgments. We must engage with different religious traditions with respect and empathy, as we recognize the historical and cultural forces that have shaped their beliefs and practices. This requires a commitment to cross-cultural understanding, which fosters a spirit of dialogue and mutual learning.

The ongoing spiritual journey also necessitates a commitment to ethical living. Our beliefs should not remain abstract ideals but be integrated into our daily lives to shape our actions and interactions with others. This involves developing compassion, empathy, and a commitment to social justice. Spiritual growth is not simply a matter of intellectual understanding or personal experience, but also of ethical action. It is about applying our spiritual insights to create a more just and compassionate world, which reflects the values and principles we hold dearly. This means actively engaging in the challenges of our time, striving to alleviate suffering, and promoting the well-being of all beings. It is about recognizing our interconnectedness and acting accordingly, and translating our beliefs into concrete actions that benefit others and the planet.

Finally, the ongoing dialogue between humanity and the Divine necessitates humility and a willingness to embrace uncertainty. The search for meaning is not a quest for definitive answers, but a journey of lifelong learning and exploration. There will be moments of doubt, confusion, and even despair, but these challenges are not obstacles to be overcome but integral aspects of the spiritual journey itself. Embracing uncertainty requires a certain level of courage, and a willingness to accept the limitations of our understanding. It involves a profound sense of humility, appreciation of the vastness of the unknown, and the mystery that surrounds us.

This humility is not a sign of weakness, but rather strength that enables us to approach the search for meaning with openness. It is also a willingness to learn and grow. The journey itself, the continuous striving to understand our place in the universe, and our relationship with the Divine, is perhaps more significant than arriving at any single conclusion. The dialogue continues to evolve, deepen, and to enrich our understanding of ourselves and the world around us. The journey is the destination.

The Importance of Reflection: Personal Insights and Applications

The preceding chapters have explored the multifaceted dialogue between humanity and the Divine. They have traversed theological landscapes, philosophical inquiries, and historical narratives. We have examined diverse perspectives, acknowledged the complexities and ambiguities inherent in this enduring conversation, but the ultimate purpose of this exploration is not simply to accumulate knowledge. Rather, it is to foster a deeper understanding of our own relationship with the transcendent; to cultivate a more meaningful and purposeful life. This final section, therefore, invites you, the reader, to engage in a crucial act of introspection—reflection. As you pursue your personal journey, integrate the insights gained throughout this book.

Reflection is not a passive activity but an active and intentional process of examining our beliefs, experiences, and values. It requires a willingness to confront our biases, challenge our assumptions, and honestly assess the foundations of our spiritual convictions. Consider the various approaches we have discussed, which help us understand the Divine: the mystical, rational, experiential, and social. Which of these resonates most deeply with your own personal experience? Where do you find points of connection, and where do you encounter tensions or discrepancies?

Perhaps you identify strongly with a particular theological tradition, or maybe your spiritual journey transcends established religious frameworks. The crucial point is not to arrive at definitive answers, but to engage in a process of honest self-assessment and to acknowledge the complexity and fluidity of your own spiritual landscape.

This self-examination can take many forms, one of them being journaling, which offers a valuable tool for reflection. As you reflect on your experiences, you also record moments of inspiration, doubt, or profound connection. When you regularly write about your thoughts and feelings, it helps you identify patterns, track your spiritual growth, and gain a clearer understanding of your evolving relationship with Divine. Contemplative practices, such as meditation or prayer, can facilitate deeper introspection, which allows you to quiet the mental chatter and access more profound level of awareness. These practices create a space for reflection and enable you to observe your thoughts and emotions without judgment. They also help to foster self-compassion and understanding. Consider incorporating these practices into your daily routine and carve out dedicated time for stillness and reflection.

You can enrich your reflective process by going beyond personal journaling and contemplative practices, to engage in meaningful conversations with others. Discuss your spiritual beliefs and experiences with trusted friends, family members, or spiritual mentors. Share your thoughts and listen to the perspectives of others to broaden your understanding, challenge your assumptions, and acquire new insights. A supportive community can provide encouragement and guidance during moments of doubt or uncertainty and foster a sense of belonging and shared purpose. The act of dialogue, where individuals share personal vulnerabilities and seek understanding, is a powerful catalyst for spiritual growth.

The application of these reflective practices extends beyond personal growth to inform how we engage with the world around us. How does your understanding of Divine influence your actions and interactions with others? Do your beliefs translate into ethical conduct, a commitment to social justice, and compassion for those who suffer? Reflect on your daily life and consider your relationships, your work, and your engagement with society. How might you integrate your spiritual insights into these spheres of life? How can you act in ways that align with your values and convictions? This integration is not a matter of imposing your beliefs on others, but rather of living authentically; embodying the principles you hold dear.

Consider the concept of "neighbor" in your own life. Who are your neighbors? Is it limited to those who live close by, or does it extend to the broader community, those in need, or to future generations?

It is crucial to reflect on the scope of our responsibility in order to translate our spiritual insights into concrete action. Consider engaging in acts of service, where you volunteer your time to causes that align with your values. You may also choose to advocate for social justice within your community. These actions are not mere charitable deeds. They are expressions of deeper spiritual commitment, a tangible demonstration of your beliefs.

The application of reflective insights also pertains to the way we interact with different belief systems and worldviews. Having engaged with the diverse perspectives presented in this book, how does this newfound awareness shape your interactions with individuals who hold different religious or spiritual beliefs? Can you approach these encounters with greater empathy and understanding, as you recognize the shared human longing for meaning and connection? Can you engage in respectful dialogue and seek common ground rather than emphasizing differences? It is a personal virtue to develop this capacity for interfaith dialogue, and a crucial component of building a more peaceful and just world.

In our increasingly interconnected world, global perspectives deserve our mindful consideration. How do the themes and concepts explored in this book resonate with the global community? How do they resonate with the diverse experiences and challenges that humanity faces?

Reflect on the interconnectedness of our world, and recognize the impact our actions have on others, regardless of geographical distance. Can you extend your compassion and concern to those beyond your immediate circle and advocate for environmental sustainability, global justice, and humanitarian aid? This global perspective adds another layer to our spiritual journey and highlights our shared humanity. It also highlights our collective responsibility for the well-being of our planet and its inhabitants.

Finally, consider the ongoing nature of the dialogue between

humanity and the Divine. This is not a quest for definitive answers but a lifelong journey of exploration and discovery. Embrace the uncertainty, the moments of doubt, and the challenges inherent in this process. These are not setbacks but integral parts of the journey, opportunities for growth and deepening understanding. Cultivate humility, as you acknowledge the limits of human knowledge and the mysteries that remain beyond our comprehension. The ongoing dialogue is not about reaching a destination but about embracing the journey itself; continually refining our understanding and striving to live a life of meaning and purpose.

This reflection invites a reassessment of your spiritual path, though it is not a call for a radical overhaul of your beliefs. This reflection is an invitation to engage in a more thoughtful and deliberate approach to your spiritual life. By integrating the knowledge and insights gained throughout this exploration, you can cultivate a deeper understanding of your relationship with the Divine, translating your convictions into meaningful actions that shape your life and contribute to the betterment of the world. The journey continues, ever evolving, and ever deepening. The dialogue remains open, awaiting your continued participation and engagement. The ongoing conversation between humanity and Divine awaits your next contribution.

Future Directions: Further Explorations of Faith and Purpose

The preceding reflections on personal introspection and the application of spiritual insights to daily life, lay the groundwork for the next crucial step: which is a commitment to ongoing intellectual and spiritual inquiry. The dialogue between humanity and the Divine is not a static conversation concluded within the pages of this book. It is a dynamic, evolving process that demands continuous engagement. This section, therefore, suggests further avenues for exploration, while encouraging a lifelong pursuit of deeper understanding and meaning.

One area that is fertile for further exploration is within the intersection of faith and science. For centuries, these two domains have generally been perceived as existing in stark opposition, with faith relegated to the realm of belief, and science confined to the empirical. However, a more nuanced perspective is emerging, which acknowledges the limitations of both approaches. It also acknowledges the potential for fruitful dialogue. Scientists are increasingly grappling with questions of origins, consciousness, and the nature of reality, and are raising inquiries that touch upon fundamental theological themes. Similarly, theologians are exploring the implications of scientific discoveries, as they integrate scientific knowledge into their understanding of the Divine and the Universe. The emerging field, "theology of science", offers a fascinating avenue for further inquiry. It also bridges the perceived gap between faith and offers a more integrated worldview.

Exploring the intersection of faith and science might involve engaging with the work of prominent scientists and theologians, who have addressed this interdisciplinary dialogue. Consider, for instance, the writings of Ian Barbour, a pioneer in the field of science and religion, who explored various models of interaction between science and religion. Examine the perspectives of scientists who have incorporated spiritual or theological considerations into their work, such as the physicist and theologian, John Polkinghorne. Explore the contributions of theologians who have attempted to reconcile scientific findings with theological doctrines and pay attention to their methodologies and arguments. This intellectual engagement will not only deepen your understanding of both science and faith but also foster a more comprehensive and integrated worldview.

Another path worthy of pursuit is a deeper exploration of various spiritual practices and traditions. While this book has touched upon several approaches to spirituality, the world's religious and spiritual traditions offer a vast and rich tapestry of practices and beliefs.

If we engage with these diverse traditions—contemplative Buddhism, mystical traditions of Sufism, the liturgical practices of Christianity, and the like—we can broaden our understanding of the human search for meaning and connection with the Divine. This engagement is not to be approached with a superficial curiosity, but with a genuine willingness to learn and appreciate the unique perspectives and practices of each tradition.

The study of comparative religion offers a valuable framework for this exploration. By carefully comparing different religious traditions, we can gain a richer appreciation for the common threads that unite them; also, the unique perspectives that distinguish them. We can also identify common themes, such as the experience of the sacred, the pursuit of ethical conduct, or the longing for ultimate reality, with a view to highlighting the shared human quest for meaning. Understanding the historical development and sociocultural contexts of these traditions add further depth to this comparative study. We need to engage with this comparative approach in order to foster a more nuanced understanding of religious diversity, challenge ethnocentric assumptions, and promote intercultural dialogue.

Furthermore, the study of ethics provides another compelling avenue for exploration. The concept of morality has been extensively explored across various religions and philosophies. How our understanding of the Divine shapes our moral compass, and how ethical frameworks influence our relationship with the Divine, becomes a crucial area of continued investigation. The exploration of ethical dilemmas, such as environmental stewardship, social justice, and the treatment of vulnerable populations, provides an opportunity to apply our spiritual insights to pressing contemporary issues. This engagement will not only enhance our ethical reasoning capabilities, but also equip us to make more informed and responsible decisions, not just within our personal lives but also in the broader social context.

The concept of purpose, deeply entwined with faith and the human condition, also warrants further investigation. The search for purpose is a fundamental human drive, which motivates us to seek meaning and direction in our lives. However, this search is rarely straightforward, and often involves navigating ambiguity, doubt, and uncertainty. Further exploration might, on purpose, delve into various philosophical perspectives, such as existentialism, nihilism, and humanism, to understand how different worldviews address the question of human purpose. It is equally important to understand the psychological and social aspects of the quest for purpose. Consider the role of community, belonging, and social contribution, in fostering a sense of purpose, as you appreciate how these factors contribute to both individual and collective well-being.

Finally, the ongoing dialogue between humanity and the Divine demands a commitment to self-reflection. The spiritual journey is not a passive pursuit, but an active and ongoing process of self-discovery and growth. Regular self-reflection, through journaling, meditation, or contemplative practices, allows us to examine our beliefs, values, and actions. It also helps to identify areas for growth and change. It is crucial to cultivate a posture of humility and openness to new perspectives, if we are to maintain this dynamic exchange with the transcendent.

In conclusion, the future of this ongoing dialogue lies in our commitment to continuous exploration. The intersection of faith and science, the study of diverse spiritual traditions, the engagement with ethical frameworks, and the relentless pursuit of self-awareness, are not peripheral aspects. They are vital components in our ongoing conversation with the transcendent. We shall not only deepen our understanding of the Divine by embarking on these paths of inquiry, but also transform our lives, and foster a deeper connection with ourselves, others, and the world around us. The journey continues, and invites further participation, reflection, and growth. The dialogue is open. Your voice matters. Your contribution is essential. The ongoing conversation awaits.

A Call to Action: Living a Life of Purpose and Meaning

The preceding reflections have, hopefully, illuminated the multifaceted nature of the ongoing dialogue between humanity and the Divine. However, the true value of such exploration lies in its transformative power to shape our lives, and not merely in intellectual understanding. This is where the call for action arises: Live a life of purpose and meaning and actively engage with the world. Also, strive to embody the values and principles we have considered.

The call is not a passive acceptance of beliefs, but a dynamic engagement; a continuous striving to align our actions with our deepest convictions.

Living a life of purpose begins with self-awareness. We must honestly assess our values and identify what truly matters to us. This involves introspection, perhaps through journaling, meditation, or simply taking quiet time to reflect. What are our passions?

What causes resonation deeply within us? What are the guiding principles that shape our decisions and actions? These questions are not easily answered, but their exploration is crucial to finding our unique path toward a meaningful life. Exploration is a process of discerning our deepest selves, a journey of self-discovery that unfolds gradually over time.

Once we have begun to identify our core values, we can then start to live in accordance with them. This may involve making difficult choices, challenging our comfort zones, and stepping outside of familiar patterns. It requires courage, resilience, and a willingness to embrace the unknown. Consider, for example, the individual deeply committed to environmental sustainability. To live this value, it might involve making conscious choices about consumption, advocating for responsible policies, or actively participating in environmental conservation efforts. Similarly, someone whose core values center on social justice might dedicate their time to volunteering in underserved communities, advocating for marginalized groups, or working to address systemic inequalities.

Living a purposeful life is not solely about grand gestures; it is also about the small, everyday actions that reflect our values. A commitment to honesty in our interactions, kindness as we deal with others, and integrity in our professional endeavors, all contribute to a life lived with purpose. These actions may seem insignificant, but once they accumulate, they form a tapestry of meaningful choices that collectively shape our character and impact the world around us. The daily practice of mindfulness, for instance, can help us be more present in our interactions, and to foster more genuine connections with those around us.

However, purpose is not a solitary pursuit as it is intrinsically linked to our relationships with others, our contribution to the larger community. Meaningful engagement with the world around us extends beyond personal fulfillment. It involves actively working to improve the lives of others, while contributing to the greater good. This could involve volunteering at a local charity, mentoring young people, or simply offering a helping hand to a neighbor in need. It could mean advocating for social change, challenging injustice, or working towards a more equitable and just society. The possibilities are as diverse as the individuals who choose to engage with the world in this way.

Furthermore, the pursuit of purpose often involves facing challenges and setbacks. This is an inherent part of human experience, And the capacity to persevere despite obstacles is crucial to maintaining a sense of direction and purpose. We need to cultivate inner strength, learn from our mistakes, and maintain a sense of hope amidst adversity, if we are to develop resilience. We can benefit from essential encouragement and guidance during challenging times, if we develop a strong support network, and connect with others who share our values and goals.

The concept of legacy is another important aspect of living a purposeful life. We all leave a mark in the world, whether we intend to or not. The question is: What kind of a mark do we want to leave? What legacy do we hope to create? This reflection can guide our actions and motivate us to make choices that will positively impact future generations. For some, this might involve contributing to a specific field of study or creating works of art that inspire others. For others, it might involve raising a family grounded in strong values or making a difference in their local communities.

The integration of spiritual practice into our daily lives can profoundly enhance our sense of purpose. Whether it is through prayer, meditation, or engagement with sacred texts, these practices can provide a sense of grounding and perspective, as well as connection to something larger than us. They can offer solace amidst challenges and provide strength and resilience in the face of adversity. The regular practice of gratitude, for instance, can significantly shift our perspective, and allow us to focus on the positive aspects of our lives while fostering a sense of contentment.

Finally, the search for purpose is not a destination but a journey. It is an ongoing process of self-discovery, growth, and adaptation. Life, inevitably, presents unexpected twists and turns, requiring us to adapt to our goals and adjust our plans accordingly. The ability to embrace change, remain flexible, and remain open to new experiences is crucial to navigating this journey successfully.

The key to maintaining a sustainable path toward meaning is to remember that our purpose might evolve over time and hence be ready to adjust to new circumstances and evolving priorities.

The dialogue between humanity and the Divine is not merely a philosophical exercise but a call to action; a summons to engage with the world and live a life that reflects our deepest values and beliefs. By striving for self-awareness, aligning our actions with our convictions, engaging with our communities, and cultivating a resilient spirit, we contribute to a richer, more meaningful life. That richer life is not just for ourselves, but for all those we touch along the way. The journey toward purpose is a lifelong endeavor, one that requires commitment, reflection, and a willingness to embrace the unpredictable nature of life. But the rewards, which entail a life lived with intention, and contribution to greater good, are immeasurable. The dialogue awaits your participation. The world awaits your contribution. Your purpose awaits your discovery.

Acknowledgments

The completion of this book has been a journey, and I am deeply grateful to the many individuals who have supported me along the way. First and foremost, I want to express my sincere gratitude to my family, whose unwavering love and patience have been my constant source of strength. Their understanding and encouragement allowed me to dedicate the time and energy necessary to this project.

I also owe a debt of gratitude to my mentor in the field of religious studies, whose insightful critiques and guidance have been invaluable in shaping my thinking and refining my arguments. The

anonymous reviewers provided invaluable feedback, and their suggestions considerably strengthened the final product. Finally, I want to acknowledge the contribution of the countless individuals who have shared their stories and insights over the years. They inspired this exploration of the human search for purpose.

Appendix

This appendix includes supplementary materials relevant to the main text. They include a selection of relevant primary source documents, such as excerpts from various religious and philosophical texts referenced in the book.

Resources for further research, including websites and academic journals, are also included, to assist readers who wish to delve deeper into the topics explored. I have also provided a comparison chart outlining the diverse approaches to achieving a sense of purpose across various religious and philosophical traditions.

Glossary

This glossary provides concise definitions of key terms and concepts used throughout the book. It aims to enhance accessibility and understanding for readers unfamiliar with theological or philosophical terminologies. Key terms such as "teleology," "eschatology," "existentialism," "deontology," "virtue ethics," and "spiritual practices", are defined with contextual relevance to the book's arguments.

References

The following list comprises the books, articles, and other sources cited within this book. Citations follow the Chicago Manual of Style, 17th Edition. This list aims to provide a comprehensive record of the research and scholarship that underpins the arguments presented herein.

A full bibliography, including works consulted but not directly cited in the text, is available upon request.

www.ingramcontent.com/pod-product-compliance
Lightning Source LLC
Chambersburg PA
CBHW021223130626
46554CB00004B/1337